THE MAKING OF
TAXI
DRIVER

Hugo hon

Don't loose the
filmaking bug.

All my love

[signature]

THE MAKING OF
TAXI
DRIVER

GEOFFREY MACNAB

The publisher wishes to thank the Book Division at Lasgo Chrysalis London
for their ongoing support in developing this series.

Published by Unanimous Ltd.
Unanimous Ltd. is an imprint of MQ Publications Ltd.
12 The Ivories, 6–8 Northampton Street, London, N1 2HY
Tel: 44 (0)20 7359 2244 Fax: 44 (0)20 7359 1616
email: mail@mqpublications.com
website: www.mqpublications.com

Printed and bound in France

ISBN: 1 90331 882 3

1 2 3 4 5 6 7 8 9

Picture credits:
Cover: © Columbia Pictures/The Kobal Collection.
Picture section: page 97 © Columbia Pictures/The Kobal Collection;
page 98 © Jack Manning/The New York Times Co./Getty Images;
page 99 © Webphoto/ Vinmag Archive Ltd.; pages 100–101 © Snap Photo
Library/Rex Features; page 102 © Columbia Pictures; pages 103, 104, and 105
© Columbia Pictures/The Kobal Collection; pages 106–107 © Fotos
International/Getty Images; page 108 © Columbia Pictures/Snap Photo Library/
Rex Features; page 109 © Columbia Pictures/Getty Images; page 110
© Columbia Pictures/Snap Photo Library/Rex Features; page 111 © Columbia
Pictures; page 112 © Columbia Pictures.

contents

introduction

"*Taxi Driver* is a cokey movie. Big pressure, short schedule, and short money, New York in the summer. Night shooting. I have only visited the set once and they are all doing blow. I don't see it. I just know it." *Taxi Driver* producer Julia Phillips in her book *You'll Never Eat Lunch in This Town Again*.

"I know that *Taxi Driver* holds up. The reason it holds up is that it is the real deal. Scorsese, Bob [De Niro] and I were in that place at that time." *Taxi Driver* screenwriter Paul Schrader, interviewed by the author, March 2005.

New York, the summer of 1975. The heat is stifling, 95 degrees in the shade. Martin Scorsese and his crew are out on the streets, shooting *Taxi Driver*. This is a movie that nobody in Hollywood holds much hope for. Columbia boss David Begelman detests the script and has only greenlit the project because producers Michael and Julia Phillips are riding on the back of the box-office success of their Oscar-winning *The Sting* (1973). The budget is small: under $2 million.

Scorsese does not care about the stifling heat or the lack of resources. He is pushing his crew to extremes. They have under two months in which to shoot the picture. The atmosphere on set is tense and chaotic. "I like my movie sets to be a madhouse, like the stateroom scene in [The Marx Brothers'] *A Night at the Opera*," the director jokes to the press. He and his team ricochet from location to location, taking in such landmarks as the Bellmore Cafeteria on 28th Street and Park Avenue South, the after-hours hangout of choice for New York cabbies; the porno theaters on 8th Avenue; the Garment district and Columbus Circle. These are all places that Scorsese, who grew up in the city, knows intimately.

Scorsese, screenwriter Paul Schrader and star Robert De Niro all approach the project with the same measure of zealotry, as if this is the most important film they are ever likely to make. "We were all young enough to want to do something that will last," Schrader later tells *Film Comment*. "De Niro told me, when we were talking about whether the film will make any money, that he felt it was a film people would be watching 50 years from now, and that whether everybody watched it next year wasn't important. That's how we came to it, and that's why we didn't make any compromises; we figure if we're going to compromise on money, we're certainly not going to compromise on anything else."

Early portents are not good. Once shooting is finished, the film is reedited repeatedly. No one much likes the rough cut on its first screening. "The film has been cut according to Schrader's script and sucks," Julia Phillips observes in typically abrasive fashion.

Begelman continues to detest the film. There are reports of raging arguments between Scorsese and Schrader. The censors are not happy with what they regard as a glorified exploitation pic. In particular, they object to the bloody shootout that ends the movie. As the cinematographer Michael Chapman admits of a sequence in which blood is spattered on walls and limbs are shot apart, this looks like a painting by abstract expressionist Robert Rauschenberg: "It was incredibly violent." To satisfy the ratings board and ensure that the film will receive an R rating, guaranteeing a mainstream release, Scorsese chooses to desaturate the colors. (The message from the censors was that he could spill as much blood as he wanted as long as he did not do it in strident red.) Perversely, Scorsese welcomes the censors' interventions: "In a way, the violence comes out more surreal and exaggerated than it was originally. I had never liked the red we got anyway, and there's something more effective about the blood with all that red toned down."

It all comes good on a cold morning in early February 1976, when *Taxi Driver* is released in New York. Schrader passes by the movie theater on the morning of the release and, to his amazement, sees queues of young men waiting to buy tickets. His initial thought is that there has been a problem with the projection and that nobody has been allowed in. In fact, the first screening is already sold out. This is the crowd for the next showing.

Disconcertingly, the young men in the line snaking around the block look disarmingly similar to the man on the poster, which shows a solitary man walking down a New York sidewalk, head bowed, hands in pockets beneath the slogan: "On every street in every city, there's a nobody who dreams of being a somebody." The moviegoers clamoring to see *Taxi Driver* on its first day on general release are drawn to the film because they are sure it is about their own lives and they have heard that there will be blood and violence. They seemingly regard it as a gory B-movie. Although the film breaks house records at the Coronet, Scorsese admits to a few misgivings about the late-night audience on the opening day. "The first show [at noon] went beautifully," he tells a press conference in Washington DC three days later. "Maybe that was a special sort of audience. The last show, at 10pm, was a little different. They seemed to be enjoying the shootout, and I didn't intend that. I intended what the first audience seemed to be feeling. I wanted a gasping, a sort of pulling back."

For an entirely different perspective on the same movie, flash forward a few months to Cannes in May 1976. Tennessee Williams, the great American playwright who created *A Streetcar Named Desire* with its archetypal macho outsider Stanley Kowalski (so memorably played by Marlon Brando in Elia Kazan's film), is president of the Cannes Film Festival jury. His fellow jurors, including English actress Charlotte Rampling and political filmmaker Costa-Gavras, are sifting through a competition that offers the usual mix of new titles from established auteurs, leavened by a few films from the brave young turks of world cinema. Wim Wenders' *Kings of the Road*, Eric Rohmer's *The Marquise of O*, Roman Polanski's *The Tenant*, and Alan Parker's *Bugsy Malone* are all in contention, but Williams and his jurors award the Palme D'Or, the festival's most prestigious prize, to *Taxi Driver*. Although Williams admits to qualms about the violence in *Taxi Driver*, that does not sway the jury's decision. For Europeans, the film sums up perfectly the seething discontents of a United States still traumatized by Vietnam and Watergate. They see it as a sociopolitical document.

Next stop, a few months farther down the line, is the 49th Academy Awards at the Dorothy Chandler Pavilion in Los Angeles. *Taxi Driver* is up for four Oscars, including Best Picture. To widespread surprise, it loses in every category. Best

Picture goes to *Rocky*, John G. Avildsen's wish-fulfillment fantasy about a long-in-the-tooth boxer (Sylvester Stallone) getting his shot at the title. The critics and many in the audience regard this as a rank injustice. The other three films in the running for Best Picture are *All the President's Men*, *Bound for Glory*, and *Network*. No one in Hollywood is in much doubt that *Taxi Driver* is the most inventive and disturbing of the nominees. They view it as an outstandingly crafted movie by a new director and as a future classic.

Exploitation pic, sociopolitical drama, Hollywood prestige picture: somehow, *Taxi Driver* manages to be all three. The filmmakers themselves cannot figure out why it plays so well or seems to have such universal appeal. "I thought at the time we were making a film that wouldn't speak to very many people. I was surprised that it had such an acceptance," Scorsese later said of a film that was a box-office hit in spite of touching on such subjects as voyeurism, teenage prostitution, vigilante violence, and political corruption. There is a sense of a film that has somehow transcended its own limitations.

To Columbia's amazement and Scorsese's evident surprise, the film does very brisk box-office. Not only is it a commercial success, making over $12 million on its initial release, but it is also fawned over by many critics. To understand just why the film exercised such a magnetic pull on audiences, it is necessary to look in a little more depth at the circumstances in which it was conceived, and to discover just how the protagonist Travis Bickle came to life.

the players

When *Taxi Driver* was in preproduction, its 32-year-old star Robert De Niro was in Italy, completing shooting on his first big international movie, *1900*. Directed by Bernardo Bertolucci, this was an epic saga about the rise of fascism in Italy. De Niro played Alfredo Berlinghieri, the son of a wealthy landowner (Burt Lancaster). Alfredo is an effete dilettante, seemingly blind to the political convulsions around him and unable to stem the ambitions of his fascistic foreman (Donald Sutherland). It is an intriguing performance precisely because it is so far removed from the stock image of De Niro as mercurial gangster or raging psychotic. Alfredo is a gentle, wistful character, with a naivety that recalls Peter Sellers' Chance the gardener in *Being There* (1979).

Even when he was filming *1900*, De Niro was preparing to play Travis Bickle in *Taxi Driver*. Every weekend, when filming finished in Rome, he would fly back to New York. "He got himself a cab driver's licence. He would go to a garage and pick up a real cab and really drive the cab around New York and then he would turn it in and fly back to Italy and work again," Peter Boyle, who played Travis's fellow cab driver Wizard, later recalled.

Meticulous research is the hallmark of De Niro's acting style. He is famous for preparing for each new role in forensic detail. When he played boxer Jake La Motta in Scorsese's later film *Raging Bull* (1980), he put on over 60 pounds in order to show La Motta as a middle-aged has-been whose career inside the ring has come to an end. For the fight sequences themselves, he was, by contrast, supremely fit. Similarly, when he was cast as the steel worker turned GI in Michael Cimino's *The Deer Hunter* (1978), he made sure he lived the character's lifestyle, even to the extent of doing shifts in a factory. In preparation for *The Godfather Part II* (1974), he decamped to Sicily to study and absorb the local speech patterns. When he was playing the gangster Jimmy Conway in Scorsese's *Goodfellas* (1990), he pestered real-life hoodlum Henry Hill, a gangster turned stool pigeon who had shopped his former associates to the authorities, for details of how James "Jimmy the Gent" Burke, the model for Conway, had behaved. De Niro was like an anthropologist. He wanted to know everything: how Burke held his whiskey glass, how he dressed, how he walked, how he smiled.

Spending hours driving around nighttime New York in a specially hired taxi might sound excessive, but for De Niro, this was simply the groundwork. He would pick up fares, chat with passengers, and immerse himself in the night and day life of the typical New York cab driver. Even before he started his masquerade, when he was still midway through the making of *1900* and confined to Italy, De Niro was already trying to come up with a way to play Travis Bickle. When he had time off, he visited a US army base in Italy so that he could meet young Midwestern GIs, tape record them, and study their speech patterns and behavior. Once *1900* was finished, he could devote a little more time to the job. "I rode around the backstreets of New York 12 hours a day for a fortnight and I guess I made around a hundred bucks a week in fares. It was hard ... I mean I really earned my money," he later confided to journalists. *Taxi Driver* scriptwriter Schrader gave the actor his boots, jacket, and trousers: another way for De Niro to flesh out the character of Travis Bickle.

Self-discipline was at the root of De Niro's working method. On the *Taxi Driver* set, like the professional thief he played so memorably 20 years later in Michael Mann's *Heat* (1995), he was cold, analytical, and invariably had every angle covered. "An actor's body is an instrument, and you have to learn to play an instrument," De Niro observed. "It is like knowing how to play the piano. There ought to be acting schools that take you in as children, the way it is done with musicians ... actors must expose themselves to the surroundings and keep their minds obsessed with that. Sooner or later, an idea will creep into your head ... a feeling, a clue, or maybe an incident will occur that the actor can later connect to the scene when he was doing it." Practice, he asserted, was paramount. Just as a musician would play the same scales again and again, De Niro would rehearse the everyday routines of the characters he was playing. "You've got to physically and mentally become that person you are portraying."

De Niro's creed was always to "look at everything" about any given character, however trivial. The key to any performance might lie in the tiniest, most throwaway detail. "The important thing is to think it all out ... sometimes I write down my ideas. The main thing is to put in the time, even if it's boring. Then you know you've covered every possibility when you make your choices."

For movie audiences and most critics, De Niro was a star who burst on the scene from nowhere. Like Scorsese, he had received one of his first big breaks from exploitation king Roger Corman, appearing opposite Shelley Winters in

Bloody Mama (1970), Corman's film about the Ma Barker clan. (He played a glue-sniffing junkie.) He had also had roles in some low-budget Brian De Palma films—*The Wedding Party* (1969), *Greetings* (1968), *Hi Mom!* (1970)—and had won his share of plaudits as a baseball player with a terminal illness in John Hancock's *Bang the Drum Slowly* (1973). "He reminds me of Alec Guinness, submerging himself totally in his role. He didn't even want to take off his baseball uniform. He lived in it," Hancock later told one interviewer. "Guinness isn't a personality actor, he's a character actor who is also a star—and that's Bobby. But he has an eroticism Guinness never had." De Palma, meanwhile, recalled him as shy and self-effacing.

Then came his turn as Johnny Boy in *Mean Streets* (1973) and as the youthful Vito Corleone in *The Godfather Part II* (1974) and his status as one of the leading film actors of his generation was assured. What is often overlooked is just how grueling an apprenticeship he served. Long before he was starring in Coppola and Scorsese films, he had studied extensively with the leading "method" drama teachers of the era, among them Stella Adler (famous as Marlon Brando's mentor), Lee Strasberg, and Luther James. He also appeared in countless off-Broadway and off-off-Broadway plays. Although Travis Bickle in *Taxi Driver* gives his age as 26, De Niro was well into his thirties when he played the role and already had a wealth of experience.

Perhaps his driven attitude toward his craft was governed by the example of his parents, both artists who took themselves intensely seriously. De Niro was born in New York's Lower East Side on August 17th, 1943. His father,

Robert De Niro Sr., was a poet and sculptor who had studied with Josef Albers and Hans Hoffmann. De Niro's mother, Virginia Admiral, had also studied with Hoffman. They were a glamorous couple, living in a loft in Greenwich Village and part of a bohemian circle that included critics like Clement Greenberg and Manny Farber (later to write an outspoken attack on *Taxi Driver*) and Anais Nin and Tennessee Williams (the president of the Cannes jury that gave *Taxi Driver* the Cannes Palme D'Or). Both exhibited their work at Peggy Guggenheim's gallery, which also helped launch the careers of Jackson Pollock and Mark Rothko. Although his parents split up not long after De Niro was born, he remained close to both of them and clearly shared their intense and unremitting commitment to their craft.

As a kid, De Niro was nicknamed "Bobby Milk," ostensibly because he was so pale. Fittingly enough for someone later to play Travis Bickle, he was known as a loner when he was growing up in New York's Little Italy, preferring to read books rather than hang around with the other children from the neighborhood. When he was 10 years old, he was cast as the cowardly lion in a school production of *The Wizard of Oz* and discovered that he was comfortable on stage. In interviews, he later confessed that he was able to express himself more easily when acting than in real life.

De Niro dropped out of high school at the age of 16. Not long afterward, he took the first steps in his professional acting career, winning a part in a production of Chekhov's *The Bear* that toured high schools on the East Coast. The early years were a struggle. He was often out of work, but he persevered. "I never became disillusioned. I knew that if I kept at it I would at least make a living," he told journalists when *Taxi Driver* received its European premiere in Cannes in 1976. "If you are halfway decent at what you do, by the law of averages, in five or ten years you will make enough money to do what you want to do."

Right from the outset of his film career, his craving for privacy was apparent. He regarded interviews as an intrusion and tried to keep his distance from the press. This, of course, magnified the mystique surrounding him. He was also fiercely resistant to being typecast and intensely suspicious about all the hoopla surrounding film stardom. De Niro was not motivated by money and had no compunctions about turning down plum studio roles. One part he was determined to play, though, was Travis Bickle.

De Niro and filmmaker Martin Scorsese had grown up on adjoining streets but did not know each other, at least by name. When they were introduced in the early 1970s, Scorsese immediately recognized the young actor. "He'd heard that I had made a film about his neighborhood— *Who's That Knocking at My Door* [1967]—though he used to hang out with a different group of people, on Broome Street, while we were on Prince Street," Scorsese recalled to journalists David Thompson and Ian Christie. The director and the young actor had several acquaintances in common. Scorsese later said that one of the main reasons he cast De Niro in *Mean Streets* (1973) was that the actor had turned up for his audition wearing "the tight hat of a Brooklyn punk ... when I saw that crazy hat, I knew he'd be perfect."

Like Scorsese, De Niro had enjoyed the hospitality of producers Julia and Michael Phillips on his forays to California to pursue a career in Hollywood. As his biographer John Baxter notes, the Phillipses' beach house was a magnet for "talented but socially inept newcomers from New York and the Midwest." Men with big egos and minimal social skills enjoyed the hedonistic parties that Michael and Julia Phillips used to throw. Pumped up with drugs and alcohol, they were able to behave like the Mr Bigs they so desperately wanted to become. De Niro, however, was an incongruous presence at such gatherings. He was too introspective and too intense to enjoy or flourish at such parties.

Travis Bickle was a leap beyond De Niro's role as Johnny Boy in Scorsese's *Mean Streets* (1973). Whereas Johnny was an extrovert street kid with many scene-stealing moments, Travis was a far more complex and troubling character: a loner from out of town who was both introverted and largely inscrutable. De Niro's challenge was to make a psychotic with racist leanings into at least a semi-sympathetic figure. As co-star Albert Brooks later put it: "You have a guy like Travis Bickle who is this very odd, despicable character, who becomes this hero." De Niro ended up giving an extraordinarily subtle performance: one containing traces of comedy (as the little man adrift in the big, bad city, Travis has his Chaplinesque moments), vulnerability, and self-pity, as well as rage and disgust.

As his collaborators attest, De Niro stayed in character throughout shooting. He rarely socialized with the other actors. If he was not needed on camera, he would remain on his own in his trailer. "He avoids all public contacts,"

Schrader said of him. "He just can't cope with it. He can't verbalize his feelings. But he knew what Travis is all about the moment he read the script. No explanation necessary."

These observations were echoed by Scorsese, who pointed out that De Niro "knew instinctively what we wanted. We all wanted the same thing. First and foremost, the urge behind this film is religious. I relate to it personally on an emotional level. It's about a guy whose feelings are repressed, and what happens in extreme cases of repression and isolation."

Travis despises Tom, the political campaign worker played by writer-filmmaker-comedian Albert Brooks. De Niro therefore kept a distance from Brooks. "He was the ultimate method actor," Brooks recalled. "Travis Bickle and my character would never have had words together and he did not want to have words together [with me] when we were between takes. He was that guy."

Nor was he especially friendly to Cybill Shepherd, who played Tom's colleague Betsy, the focus of Travis's lust. Some accounts suggest that he made a pass at her, was rejected, and therefore ignored her for the rest of the shoot. Others say that he did not rate her acting ability and therefore kept his distance. "Bobby treated people badly if they were not up to snuff," a collaborator later attested.

For Scorsese, De Niro was both muse and catalyst. The director (who first worked with De Niro on 1973's *Mean Streets*) knew he had found an actor who could match his own intensity and project on screen the anger, vulnerability, and warped humor that characterized Travis Bickle. These were all traits that Scorsese himself clearly shared.

Venerable British director Michael Powell—whose films such as *The Red Shoes* (1948), *The Tales of Hoffman* (1951), and *Peeping Tom* (1960) were a formative influence on the youthful Scorsese—memorably describes the febrile, asthmatic New York-born filmmaker as "a gifted porcupine" and as "a pale fanatic [with] eyes that burn and a close-clipped black beard." Meeting Scorsese in London's Ladbroke Grove was, Powell suggested, akin to encountering a "twister in Kansas." "He talked a mile a minute, his mouth full of exclamations, explanations, opinions, questions, and contradictions. He was short and dynamic. He gave out energy. He had eyes like a snake, seeing everything, adopting and discarding in the same moment."

Scorsese really did have a touch of the crazed Jesuit priest about him. He was born in November 1942 in Long Island, New York. His parents were strict Catholics. Young Marty grew up in Little Italy, frail and asthmatic. Movies were an escape for a youngster not robust enough to take part in the rough and tumble of life on the streets or in the school yard. "Films are like having a person around," he told the New York *Times* in an interview in the mid-1970s. "And to have films so much a part of your life that you can't live without them is kind of nice, and I thought that's what I want to achieve for other people [as a filmmaker]."

As few profiles of the filmmaker fail to mention, Scorsese briefly harbored ambitions of joining the priesthood. In the late 1950s, he had studied at seminary school, eventually flunking out. When his dreams of the priesthood were dashed, he went to high school in the Bronx instead. Here, he became obsessed by the celluloid muse. "I was seeing many different films from all over the world," he later recalled. Ingmar Bergman's *The Seventh Seal* (1957), Sergei Eisenstein's *Alexander Nevsky* (1938), Carol Reed's *The Third Man* (1949), and Federico Fellini's work were early obsessions. He discovered Orson Welles's *Citizen Kane* (1941) on TV when he was a teenager. Even before he understood film technique, he tried to analyze why he liked certain films and would draw favorite scenes.

His high-school grades were not good enough to get him into Jesuit college. Instead, he enrolled at Washington Square College, where he began to study liberal arts. The only course about filmmaking was "The History of Motion Pictures, Television, and Radio," taught on Thursday afternoons. The teacher was a strict disciplinarian ("almost like the marine sergeant in *Full Metal Jacket* [1987]," Scorsese recalled) who quickly evicted any students who regarded film history as an easy option. Scorsese was inspired to have found a professor as passionate (and as serious) about cinema as he was.

These were heady times for filmmaking. "Cinema was being reinvented every afternoon ... it was a great time to be a film lover," Scorsese remembered. Not only were Italians like Fellini, Antonioni, Olmi, and Pasolini beginning to carve out international reputations, but this was also the heyday of the French New Wave. Scorsese was immediately smitten by the work of Godard, Truffaut, Rivette, et al. Another early influence was John Cassavetes, the director of *Shadows* (1961) and now widely acknowledged as the founding father of US independent cinema.

Scorsese uses an intriguing mix of metaphors to describe his cinephilia. Sometimes (predictably) he likens cinema to religion, but he also has more noxious points of comparison. One of his favorite quotes is by Frank Capra: "film is a disease ... when it infects your bloodstream, it takes over as the number one hormone; it bosses the enzymes, directs the pineal glands, plays Iago to your psyche. As with heroin, the antidote to film is more film."

The comparison has a distinctly personal resonance for a filmmaker whose own problems with drugs in the late 1970s are well chronicled. Like Travis Bickle himself, Scorsese is a seething, contradictory personality whose attitude toward Hollywood combines reverence with iconoclasm and disgust. He speaks constantly of the battle between "personal expression" and "commercial imperatives" that any filmmakers with their own visions must always fight within the studio system. He talks about "smuggling" his stories past the watchful eyes of studio chiefs whose only concern is the bottom line, and of the "split personality" his battles with the studios have given him.

It was a small miracle that a young Italian-American from a working-class family was able to get a foothold in the film industry at all, let alone establish himself so quickly as a director. As journalist Pete Hammill notes in his New York memoir/social history *Downtown*, Little Italy of the 1950s and 1960s did not provide its young citizens with much of a passport to anywhere. The high-school dropout rate for Italian-American kids was higher than that for the poorest blacks and Latinos. Education was frowned on by many in the community. There were few role models outside Frank Sinatra and Joe Di Maggio. "[Politician] Mario Cuomo had yet to emerge as a public figure of eloquence and passion.

Martin Scorsese and Francis Coppola were still in the dreaming stages of their careers as movie directors. Even teachers seemed to consider the Italian-American kids as 'hopeless cases who with the best of luck might pass the civil service test for the sanitation department,'" states Hammill.

As far as Scorsese's own unlikely blossoming as an auteur was concerned, it helped that in the 1960s, there emerged on the market a series of cheap, lightweight cameras such as the 16mm Arriflex. These allowed a new generation of filmmakers to create their own movies. Scorsese began to direct shorts in 1963. His first film, nine minutes long, was called *What's a Nice Girl Like You Doing in a Place Like This?*. At this stage, Scorsese, still living with his parents, thought that his real skill lay in making comedies. In 1965, while still a student, he started working on what would eventually become his first feature, *Who's That Knocking at My Door* (1968).

What Scorsese wanted to do was to capture the reality of his own life growing up in Little Italy in the same way that Fellini had portrayed the angst and boredom of the young men growing up in small-town Italy in *I Vitelloni* (1953). Scorsese's film was made in black and white with equipment borrowed from New York University and a budget scraped together in any way the director could. He was using some of the same New York locations where *Taxi Driver* would shoot a few years later. He entered an early version to the New York Festival (which had shown his shorts), but it was turned down. Already, Scorsese was experimenting with elaborate camera movements and stylized, slow-motion violence.

The director was nothing if not tenacious. As he waited to complete the picture, Scorsese attended more film courses and began to work in dogsbody jobs for filmmakers like Michael Wadleigh, a tutor at NYU's summer schools who later employed Scorsese as an editor on *Woodstock* (1970),and the Maysles brothers, pioneers of cinéma vérité documentary. To do an old student a favor, Wadleigh agreed to shoot extra footage for *Who's That Knocking at My Door*. In 1967, it screened at the Chicago Festival, where it was favorably reviewed by the young critic Roger Ebert. As Ebert's perceptive review noted of the film (which he saw under its original title *I Call First*), Scorsese managed to reconcile two schools of US filmmaking often considered to be mutually exclusive. On the one hand, the critic pointed out, this was a naturalistic character study in the vein of Elia Kazan's *On the Waterfront* (1954) or Arthur Miller's play *A View from the Bridge*: "a sincere attempt to function at the level where real lives are led." On the other, it was quirky and experimental. Scorsese, still only in his mid-twenties, was prepared to take risks and to use "improvised dialog ... hidden and handheld cameras in an attempt to capture the freshness of a spontaneous experience."

Despite Ebert's enthusiasm, Scorsese struggled to find a distributor, but he had influential admirers. Cassavetes was eventually shown the film by Scorsese's friend, *Time* magazine critic Jay Cocks, and was hugely enthusiastic. So was Roger Corman, who would soon give the young director a break by hiring him to make *Boxcar Bertha* (1972).

In 1973 came *Mean Streets*, the best calling card any director could have. Set in New York's Little Italy but largely shot in Los Angeles on a budget of only $600,000, this was a blistering gangster film that was also a parable about friendship and growing up in the big city. The film made Scorsese's reputation, but it did not make him money. Despite rave reviews at the 1973 New York Festival and in Cannes, Warner Bros bungled its release, and it was eclipsed by the other big studio movies of the time, *A Clockwork Orange* (1971), *Deliverance* (1972), and *The Exorcist* (1973) among them.

One man impressed by *Mean Streets* was Paul Schrader, the writer of *Taxi Driver*. Like the director and star, he was a driven and intense young cinephile with a very dark side. "Travis Bickle is me," Schrader liked to boast. On the face of it, this is a preposterous assertion. Bickle is the ultimate urban loner: a 26-year-old with limited education who claims he is a Vietnam veteran and who lives in his own self-enclosed world. In the early 1970s, Schrader, by contrast, was an academic and former film critic from a strict religious background. Nonetheless, both men shared the same confessional urge and the same outsider's ambivalence toward the fleshpots of New York.

It is hard to trace Travis Bickle's genealogy from the film itself. Schrader deliberately withholds almost all personal information about him. In one scene, Travis writes to his parents, apologizing for not giving his address, but we do not know where those parents live or what they do. The records about the screenwriter are much easier to access. An American of Dutch-German extraction, Schrader was born in Grand Rapids, Michigan, in 1946. His Calvinist parents were so suspicious of the corrupting power of the media that he did not see his first films until he was a teenager, nor did his family have a television. "Television was what broke the community down," Schrader suggests. The family lived in an area that was primarily Polish-Catholic. His mother discovered that after school, he was going over to a Catholic neighbor's house to watch TV. "They had a Madonna on top of the television. When she [my mother] found out that we were watching TV with a Madonna on top of the TV, she said we'll get one."

Nonetheless, he knew all about guns. His family may have been strict Calvinists, but that did not stop them from hunting. His uncles all had hunting rifles and hunting dogs. "My father was not a hunter himself, but most of the adult men would go deer hunting every fall," Schrader says.

For the young boy, growing up in Michigan, hell was not an abstract concept. Religion was taken very seriously. Every Sunday, after the sermon, his uncles would meet up at the house and discuss what the minister had said. As Schrader later recalled: "We believed in a very real hell and very real evil. My mother took my hand once and stabbed me with a needle. I went 'ow!' She said to me, 'You know how that felt, when the needle hit your thumb? Well, hell is like that ... all the time!'"

This background partly explains the obsession with religion, death, and violence that has run through all Schrader's work. It is an obsession shared by his older brother Leonard Schrader (also a filmmaker). Asked once in an interview why the brothers were so interested in the dark side of American life, Leonard replied: "It's the wrong question. You should ask why other filmmakers aren't interested. My answer is that I'm interested in America. If you're interested in the real America, the real America has got a lot of blood in the soil."

Paul Schrader had begun his studies at Calvin College, a seminary in Michigan, but had gradually become obsessed by cinema. "I became interested in movies because they were not allowed," he later said. Pauline Kael, the chief reviewer at *The New Yorker*, met him and helped him to get into UCLA Film School in Los Angeles. After graduating, he enrolled at the American Film Institute. Kael tried to fix him up with a job as a critic (there were potential openings on newspapers in Seattle and Chicago), but Schrader decided to stay in Los Angeles to try to make the grade as a scriptwriter. His first effort, *Pipeliner*, written in 1971, was never produced, but at least helped to get Schrader's name noticed by agents. It was a downbeat tale about a dying man who, as Schrader told *Film Comment*, "goes home to northern Michigan for sympathy and ends up fucking up the lives of everybody around him."

As his private life began to unravel, Schrader felt more and more like the protagonist of *Pipeliner*. His marriage broke up, but shortly afterward, so did the relationship that had caused the marriage to fail. He was on his own. His once burgeoning career as a film critic had stalled after he panned *Easy Rider* (1969) and fell out with his former mentor, Kael, when he did not take the critic's job she had lined up for him. In 1972, he was just one of a small army of would-be screenwriters trying to make it in Hollywood.

"At the time I wrote *Taxi Driver*, I was very suicidal," Schrader later claimed. "I fell into a hole of depression. I started drinking and wandering. You know how you can fall into a hole? Well, I fell into one." When he first began to dream up Travis Bickle, Schrader was homeless, debt-ridden, drifting around, living in a car, drinking himself into a stupor, hiding away in porno movie theaters. "The metaphor of taxi cab occurred to me as metaphor of male drifting loneliness," he said. "In Los Angeles I was not unlike Travis Bickle: a bundle of tightly wrapped contradictions, driving around, trying but unable to belong."

At the peak of his depression, Schrader had a bleeding gastric ulcer. "I had huge pain in my stomach ... in the hospital, I had the idea for *Taxi Driver*, because I thought that was what I am. I wrote the script rather quickly and then I took off for about six months, traveled around the country, visited old friends, and got my mental health back." Schrader completed two drafts of the screenplay in 10 days. "It [the script] jumped out at me like an animal."

For Schrader, Travis Bickle was not a one-off. Throughout his subsequent work as a writer and director, he would continue to explore the plight of the loner. "I have been drawn to a certain character: a person, usually male, who drifts on the edge of urban society, always peeping, looking into the lives of others. He'd like to have a life of his own but doesn't know how to get one," he wrote in the introduction to his collected screenplays. For Schrader, there is a through-line linking Travis Bickle with the Armani-clad, thirtysomething male prostitute played by Richard Gere in *American Gigolo* (1980) and the fortysomething drug dealer played by Willem Dafoe in *Light Sleeper* (1992).

There are also traces of Travis Bickle found in other characters Schrader has written. His films abound in condemned and lonely men or women trying to escape their fate. In *Cat People* (1982), Irena (Nastassia Kinski) famously ends up behind bars, a human captive in a panther's body in a New Orleans zoo. In *Patty Hearst* (1988), Natasha Richardson's heiress is entrapped by the revolutionaries who kidnap her, but is also a prisoner of her background.

Martyrs likewise feature prominently in his oeuvre. Think of the washed-up boxer Jake La Motta (Robert De Niro) pounding his head against his cell wall in *Raging Bull* (1980) or of the savior on the cross in *The Last Temptation of Christ* (1988). Whether or not someone as odd and as psychopathic as Travis Bickle can be called a martyr, he certainly shares that morbid tendency toward introspection that characterizes so many of Schrader's protagonists.

Scorsese and Schrader were unlikely partners. The former was a Catholic with a flamboyant and expressionistic visual sense and a relish for Grand Guignol-style bloodfest. The latter was an introspective Calvinist whose visual tastes tended toward minimalism (his favorite director was the famously spare Robert Bresson) and who was preoccupied with death and damnation.

Although they may have bickered during the making of *Taxi Driver*, the two men subsequently acknowledged that their differences made their collaborations rich and distinctive. "I think that what makes the film so vivid is that we both have essentially the same background—a kind of closed society Christian morality, though mine is rural and protestant and his is urban and catholic," Schrader commented in the book *Schrader on Schrader*.

Like many angry, macho men, Scorsese and Schrader both had their sentimental sides. This tendency found its focus in the character of Iris, the 12-year-old hooker. A doe-eyed ingenue who just happens to be turning tricks on the streets of New York, Iris is a character whose origins can be traced all the way back to the fiction of Charles Dickens via the films of D.W. Griffith. As an archetype, she is not so far removed from the similarly long-suffering, similarly precocious waif adrift in London's opium-glazed, mist-shrouded Limehouse played by Lillian Gish in Griffith's *Broken Blossoms* (1919). The success of *Taxi Driver* depended on casting a young actress who was not Pollyanna-ish, but still had a certain innocence about her. Jodie Foster proved the perfect choice.

Foster's performance was closely modeled on that of a (once) real-life teen prostitute, credited as Garth Avery. Her sunglasses, her way of talking (Iris is part child, part hustler), and even her eating habits (like all junkies, she had a sweet tooth) were inspired by the woman Schrader met by chance. This woman was hired as a consultant and even given a bit part as Iris's friend. We see her with sunglasses on and a cigarette hanging from her mouth pulling Iris away when Travis's cab almost crashes into her.

As Foster later recalled, the filmmakers' hopes that she would immediately strike up a rapport with Garth Avery were a little far-fetched. At the time of *Taxi Driver*, Foster was a 12-year-old child actress. She had grown up in a sheltered background with a fiercely protective mother. By all accounts, she was well adjusted, outgoing, a bit of a tomboy. She had so little in common with Avery that they might have been born on different planets.

Scorsese had first run into Foster at an audition in 1974. (She ended up being cast as Audrey in Scorsese's *Alice*

Doesn't Live Here Anymore (1974).) "In came this little girl with a Lauren Bacall voice. She cracked us up," Scorsese told *Time* magazine.

At first, Foster's mother was appalled that Scorsese could be so tasteless as to offer her daughter a role as a child prostitute. When mother and daughter finally agreed that Jodie would do the movie, Jodie was required to endure a lengthy session with a psychiatrist, who had to rule that she was mentally fit to endure the rigors of her role. As Foster put it, he was there "to see if I was normal enough to play a kid hooker." Her older sister was enlisted as her body double for the more graphic moments, for instance the queasy sequence in which Iris tries to pull down Travis's zipper.

In a youthful attempt at method actor-style diligence, Jodie spent a few weeks of her summer vacation in hotpants and platform shoes, walking up and down the streets of Manhattan's Lower East Side.

Studio hype had long portrayed Foster as a child genius. Her mom, former press agent Brandy Foster, had split up with her husband in 1962 when Brandy was four months pregnant with Jodie. The newborn was able to speak at the age of nine months and read by the time she was three. Almost from the outset, her mother (who had once wanted to be an actress herself) was guiding Jodie's career. There was an economic imperative for putting her daughter to work: the family needed the money.

When Jodie was still a toddler, she accompanied her brother to an audition and was talent spotted by advertising execs, who used her as the face of a nationwide campaign for Coppertone suntan lotion. The iconic Coppertone image of a dog pulling at a girl's swimsuit had a very different connotation in 1970s America than it had had in the 1950s, when an artist called Joyce Ballantyne Brand had first dreamed up the image, using her daughter as the model. As Schrader was to admit in an interview with author Kevin Jackson, "a few years ago, they did a study about incitement to rape, and one of the things that cropped up most often was the old Coppertone suntan oil ad—it had a little puppy tugging at a girl's swimsuit. It had just the right mix for these rapists of adolescent sexuality, female nudity, rear entry, animals, violence ..."

There had long been something disingenuous about Hollywood's treatment of childhood sexuality. Look at old stills of Shirley Temple, for instance in *Kid in Africa* (1932), and it is startling how similarly dressed the actress is to Iris in *Taxi Driver*. As *Sight and Sound* magazine noted in an article about "the Lolita syndrome" (June 1994), there were many instances of either older stars (for example, Mary Pickford) playing youthful, virginal teenage ingenues, or of young actresses playing the nymphet. Foster and such actresses as Sue Lyon in Stanley Kubrick's *Lolita* (1962) or Brooke Shields as the child prostitute in Louis Malle's *Pretty Baby* (1978) were examples of the latter trend.

When novelist Graham Greene wrote a review of Temple's 1937 film *Wee Willie Winkie* (directed by Scorsese's great favorite John Ford) in the magazine *Night and Day*, in which he talked about her "neat and well-developed rump" and referred to her as "a complete totsy," 20th Century-Fox was indignant. Studio lawyers soon put Greene and *Night and Day* in the docks for libel. Greene, it was claimed, had all but accused the studio of "procuring Miss Temple for immoral purposes." In his autobiography *Ways of Escape*, Greene argued that he had simply suggested that Temple had "a certain adroit coquetry that appealed to middle-aged men."

The "beastly libel," as Fox's lawyers called it, forced *Night and Day* into bankruptcy. It was a measure of how Hollywood had changed by the mid-1970s that the portrayal of the 12-year-old prostitute by one of Disney's biggest child stars ended up winning Foster an Oscar nomination. Scorsese received threatening letters ("if Jodie Foster wins for what you made her do, you will pay for it with your life," read one typical example) and had to be accompanied to the awards ceremony by FBI agents. Nonetheless, the scandal was far less severe (at least initially) than might have been anticipated. This was partly because of Foster's superb performance. It was also surely attributable to the filmmakers' decision to make Iris's pimp a white man and to the fact that those who have abused Iris receive such a grim and bloody comeuppance.

Schrader and Scorsese must have realized the implications in casting Foster as Iris. Although most of her earlier parts had been in Disney films or TV shows like *Paper Moon* (a short-lived spin-off from the film starring Foster's fellow child actress Tatum O'Neal), *Taxi Driver* was not just another film that she could innocently brush off. For better or worse, Iris was bound to become one of the defining roles in her career.

While Foster was a young actress on the up, her co-star Cybill Shepherd seemed to be heading rapidly in the opposite direction. By the time *Taxi Driver* was shot,

Shepherd's stock had fallen. She was the protégée of director Peter Bogdanovich and had starred in Bogdanovich's brilliant *The Last Picture Show* (1971) as Jacy Farrow, the beautiful, small-town girl who becomes the object of lust for two childhood friends, Sonny (Timothy Bottoms) and Duane (Jeff Bridges). A golden-haired former beauty queen and *Vogue* model with a toothsome smile and lambent skin, Shepherd was used again and again in films as an idealized fantasy figure: the 1970s Hollywood version of the beautiful princess. Filmmakers were so obsessed by her looks that they neglected to see if she could act. After *The Last Picture Show*, her career threatened to unravel. Bogdanovich, by then her lover, had cast her in *Daisy Miller* (1974) and *At Long Last Love* (1975), both disastrous flops. She was held in such low esteem the Columbia bosses did not want her in *Taxi Driver*, even in a role as small as Betsy. Her personal life was in disarray, too. Although she was still with Bogdanovich, she had also begun another affair.

There are many conflicting stories as to why she was cast. Julia Phillips has suggested that Scorsese "picked Cybill for her ass, a retro Italian gesture." Phillips, like De Niro, had extreme misgivings about Shepherd's acting ability and has written a barbed account of how bad she was in the scene in which Travis takes Betsy to a cafe.

Shepherd had not even wanted the role. Her first reaction after reading *Taxi Driver* was to throw the script across the room. "I was insulted to be offered such a nothing part," she complained. However, Scorsese needed a blonde and she needed a role in a successful film. It was all too predictable that both parties would compromise. In later years, she claimed she had been keen to do the movie all along, and that she would have "paid" to get the part. While Shepherd did not comment about the rumors that De Niro treated her badly, she did admit (a little cryptically) how "frightening and convincing" he was "once he started to lose it." She suggested he was so "believable" that he half scared her to death.

The irony about Shepherd is that, seen today, her performance seems assured and perfectly judged. Just as Travis represents the darkness, the underbelly of American life, Betsy, in her flowing Geoffrey Beene white dress, radiates cheerfulness and optimism. Like Gwyneth Paltrow a generation later, she is the golden girl. The camera seems fixated by her. Every time she ruffles her hair or its tresses blow in the breeze, the moment is framed in fetishistic close-up. The extraordinary slow-motion sequence in which Travis watches her walking into her office across a sun-filled street (with Scorsese as an extra crouching, gremlin-like, in the background), is filmed almost as if it is a shampoo commercial. We see her with Travis's fawning eyes; she is supposed to be a fantasy figure.

Shepherd preferred the scene at the end of the movie, when she climbs into Travis's cab for the last time. "It was only me, sitting in the back, Scorsese, the cinematographer, the sound man, and De Niro in the front, driving around New York. I loved being in that small space, that sense of intimacy."

Part of the project of *Taxi Driver* is to drag Betsy down into Travis's subterranean world. De Niro's biographer, John Baxter, suggests Scorsese was using Shepherd to gratify his own sexual obsessions. She has spoken about how distressing she found the scene in which Travis takes Betsy to an all-night porno theater to watch a blue movie. "He shot it in a real porno movie house on 42nd Street, late at night," Shepherd later recalled. "I had to have bodyguards because of the crazies on the streets. I'm overwhelmingly repulsed by pornography anyway, and for five or ten minutes, I was sure, I knew, that asking me to make the picture was just another way of humiliating me."

Given that Travis is set on rubbing Betsy's nose in the dirt, Scorsese may simply have been doing everything he could to ensure that he elicited a convincing response from Shepherd. Whatever the case, the "date" between Betsy and Travis is one of the strangest scenes in the film. As they walk toward the movie theater, they come across a sinister-looking drummer (Gene Palmer) with boot polish in his hair, rattling out some music on the sidewalk. For a moment or two, Travis and Betsy look like a typical, bourgeois couple. "Have a nice day?" he asks her. "Not particularly," she replies. He is in a tie and a corduroy jacket and looks almost respectable. She is in a tight-fitting white dress.

It does not take long to realize that something is amiss. Travis (obtusely) has just given Betsy a Kris Kristofferson record that she recommended to him. (He does not seem to realize that she is bound to have it already.) When she asks him if he has listened to it, he comes up with an absurd story about his record player being broken. "I was thinking, you know, maybe we could listen to it on your record player," he pleads. Moments later, as the street drummer continues to make his din, Travis drags Betsy into the double bill of two "exciting adult hits," *Sometime Sweet Susan* and the "explicit! provocative!" *Swedish Marriage Manual*. There are hookers lurking in the dimly lit lobby of the Lyric theater. Betsy allows Travis to talk her into entering, but it does not take long for her gorge to rise as she watches the biological footage of sperm and eggs intercut with a couple making love. The cinema is not crowded, but there are still "tuts!" and "hushes!" from the mainly black clientele as Betsy makes her hurried exit.

"Taking me to a place like this is about as exciting to me as saying let's fuck!" Betsy remonstrates with Travis, who has followed her out. To begin with, the scene plays like a perverse comedy, but when Travis grabs Betsy's hand and tries to make her stay, the mood darkens. The hookers look on impassively as she jumps in a cab and is driven off.

Throughout *Taxi Driver*, Shepherd's clean-living campaign worker Betsy is counterpointed with Harvey Keitel's Sport, a sleazy, low-life pimp, preying on young girls. One is light, the other darkness. While Betsy tries to sell the presidential candidate to dubious would-be voters, Sport is offering underage sex to anyone who will pay.

Keitel was almost a caricature of the method actor. He took his craft so seriously that his approach left even De Niro looking like a dilettante. A former marine, he brought the same intensity to his roles as he once did to his soldiering. Again and again, he has mentioned a piece of advice given to him by a Marine instructor in boot camp. "You're scared of this darkness because you're scared of what you don't know," the instructor told him. "I'm going to teach you to know the darkness." Knowing the darkness is precisely what Keitel's performances have been about.

Like Scorsese and De Niro, Keitel had grown up in a rough part of New York City. Born in 1947, he was a Polish Jew from a working-class family in Brooklyn. (His parents ran a refreshment stand on Brighton Beach.) Like De Niro, he was an interviewer's nightmare. "What's there to say? I had it no easier or harder than anyone else," was his stock response when asked about his background or the difficult years he spent in the mid-1960s, trying to establish himself as an actor. However, he did admit that James Dean and Marlon Brando were his inspirations.

Court stenographer, shop assistant, and salesman in a women's shoe store were some of the jobs he took before, in 1967, he answered a newspaper ad and ended up being cast as the lead, J.R., in what would become Martin Scorsese's debut feature, *Who's That Knocking at My Door* (1968). To connoisseurs of Keitel's subsequent performances, his role here seems just a little anomalous. He is clean-cut, with a naive, wistful air and a love of women and of movies. At times, he seems like a New York version of Antoine Doinel (Jean-Pierre Leaud), the hapless but immensely likable French protagonist in a number of François Truffaut's films.

At the time Keitel first met Scorsese, he had precious little acting experience. He had endured one season of summer stock and had made a number of appearances in off-off Broadway plays, including Sam Shepard's *Up to Thursday*. Like De Niro, he had also begun to study at the Actors Studio, absorbing the teachings of the legendary Lee Strasberg.

Keitel and De Niro were friends who clearly respected one another's work. Nonetheless, there is a sense that the latter usurped the former's place in Scorsese's affections. Early on, it had always been Scorsese's intention to cast Keitel as Travis Bickle. Their association already stretched back a long way. Keitel had appeared as a playboy with a mean streak in *Alice Doesn't Live Here Anymore* (1974) as well as in *Mean Streets* (1973).

When De Niro won the role as Travis, Scorsese offered Keitel the part of the campaign manager as consolation. The actor turned it down and asked to play the pimp instead. Even though he lobbied for the part and ended up giving a superb performance, Keitel had severe misgivings about Sport's relationship with Iris. One of the ironies about *Taxi Driver* was that Jodie Foster was one of the few members of the cast who did not seem troubled by the morbidity and warped sexuality at the core of the story. The older actors were far more nervous than she was about her playing a preteen prostitute who caters to the demands of New York men. Playing the pimp, Harvey Keitel could not help complaining that he felt "like a dirty old man with a little girl." Slowly, though, he found a way to relate to a character who at first glance seemed loathsome and exploitative.

Keitel, who was then living in New York's Hell's Kitchen district, spent three weeks with a real pimp, doing improvisations in which he would play the prostitute and the pimp would treat him a certain way. Then, they would switch roles. "One day, he [the pimp] said, 'I don't mistreat my girls. I love them.' I was stunned to hear that," Keitel told *Uncut* magazine. "At first I genuinely did not understand what he was talking about and I was too nervous to admit I didn't know what he was saying. Then I started understanding that there was real love involved in what he did for a living. He was taking care of the girls the way he would take care of someone that he loved. Once I got that, it was possible for me to have a relationship with the character I was playing."

Once Keitel had found the key to the role, Scorsese accommodated him—even if it meant "violating" the original screenplay. For Schrader, it was crucial that *Taxi Driver* was seen from Travis's point of view. His tunnel vision of New York gave the film its claustrophobic feel, its sense of impending apocalypse, and its stylistic unity. However, Scorsese included one improvised scene in which Sport is seen dancing with Iris. Earlier he has been shown pulling her forcibly out of Travis's taxi, but for a few brief instants, the pimp emerges in a more favorable light. He seems really to care for the 12-year-old whose body he has been selling to all-comers. Keitel later admitted that the monolog he whispers to her was based on the singing style of R&B star Barry White.

In his white vest, with his long black hair and black hat, Keitel's Sport has an unlikely comic dimension. In his first encounter with Travis, he stands in the doorway, fidgeting, wisecracking, dabbing at his mouth with a white handkerchief. "Officer, I swear I'm clean," he jokes when Travis approaches him, holding out his hands as if he expects to be handcuffed. Once he has surmised that Travis is not a cop in disguise, he runs down Iris's charms—and the personal services she offers—in loathsome detail, as if he is a fairground hustler. "$15 15 minutes, $25 half an hour ... if you wanna save yourself some money, don't fuck her. You'll be back here for some more because she's twelve and a half years old. You ain't never had no pussy like that. You can do anything you want, cum on her, fuck her in the mouth, fuck her in the ass. Cum on her face, man. She'll get your cock so hard she'll make it explode ... but no rough stuff!"

The scenes between De Niro and Keitel are riveting. Two brilliant actors are pushing each other, trying to face one another down. Critic David Thompson puts it best in his *Biographical Dictionary of Cinema* when he points out that Keitel's performance would have been drooled over had it not been for the fact that De Niro was even better. "But maybe he wouldn't have been without Keitel. For Harvey provoked Bobby, punched him, the way La Motta helped define Ray Robinson's greatness. De Niro had to be quicker, wilder, deeper, more vulnerable ... Keitel could see that he faced De Niro for the rest of his life—there might be dreams of murder in our imaginary movie. Consciously, or subconsciously, he became a touch more wilful, lonely, and dangerous."

The central performances galvanize and define *Taxi Driver*. De Niro, Keitel, and Foster are superb. However, Scorsese, like all great filmmakers, is equally interested in the minor characters and in what is happening at the edge of the frame. He takes painstaking care to cast even the smallest roles appropriately. In his films, character actors flourish. They know that he will always register even subtle and seemingly throwaway details in their performances.

In *Taxi Driver*, for example, Peter Boyle gives a fine performance as Wizard, Travis's fellow cab company employee and the closest person he has to a friend. Whereas

Travis is prey to demons, Wizard is grounded, humorous, philosophical, and has a yen for telling dirty stories, most of which he mangles in the recounting. In one key scene, Wizard tries to give Travis some advice to pull him back from the brink of his psychosis.

Scorsese allowed Boyle to improvise some of his dialog. "Go on, get drunk, get laid, do anything," Wizard tells Travis as he stands leaning on a cab outside the Belmore cafeteria. "Cause you've got no choice anyway. We're all fucked ... more or less." Wizard, we learn, has been a cabbie for 17 years, but still cannot afford his own car. He is resigned to the fact that he cannot escape the daily grind of his job. "That's about the dumbest thing I've ever heard," Travis responds after listening to this homespun philosophy, but he is smiling. For just a moment, the "bad thoughts" in his head seem to have dissipated. "I'm not Bertrand Russell, but what do you want? I'm a cabbie," Wizard protests at being mocked. "What do I know. I don't even know what the fuck you are talking about."

A bulky, balding figure, Boyle was best known to 1970s audiences as the monster in Mel Brooks' horror spoof *Young Frankenstein* (1974). He was a character actor who never made the graduation to leading man status. (Disastrously for his career, he turned down the role of Popeye Doyle in *The French Connection* (1971) because he did not want to be in a film that glamorized violence.) Nonetheless, he gave consistently inventive performances in unsung parts in some of the best films of the era. Bizarrely, before embarking on a career as an actor, he had been a monk in the Christian Brothers Order. (Like so many other of the protagonists behind *Taxi Driver*, he had a strong religious background.) "I went through that adolescent crisis where you either jump into the river or jump into spirituality. I felt the call for a while," he later said of his brief flirtation with monastic life. Once he had left religious orders, he moved to New York and lived the time-honored life of the struggling actor. He was an accomplished comedian, but was also capable of playing sad and sinister figures, for instance the racist patriarch in Marc Forster's 2002 Oscar winner *Monster's Ball*.

As a counterweight to De Niro's Travis, Scorsese cast Albert Brooks as Tom, Betsy's fellow campaign worker. This was Brooks's first film role. A facetious, pedantic, middle-class yuppie first seen counting campaign buttons, Tom Footer is the utter antithesis to Travis. The two men detest each other on sight, not only because they are both keen on Betsy, but also because they recognize that they come from such different places.

"I probably got *Taxi Driver* because Scorsese was a fan of my comedy," Brooks later admitted to *Film Comment*. His short films for TV shows like *Saturday Night Live* had long since attracted a cult following. He specialized in playing smug, slightly pompous figures who just did not seem to realize how absurd they were. His characters were often humiliated: witness the scene in *Broadcast News* (1987) in which he is shown reading the news with huge pools of sweat forming at his armpits, or the scene in *Taxi Driver* where he is clearly terrified when Travis comes into the office swinging his fists. Brooks was later to become a respected filmmaker in his own right and would return the faith that Scorsese had in casting him in *Taxi Driver* by giving his former mentor a role (as himself) in his 1999 satire *The Muse*. (This was a *Taxi Driver* reunion of sorts; Brooks also cast Cybill Shepherd.)

Even the tiniest roles were played by actors who could carry an entire film on their own. The Puerto Rican-born Victor Argo is barely on screen for a minute. He plays Melio, the storekeeper who is held up by a young black kid. To the kid's misfortune, Travis Bickle also happens to be in the store. Travis guns the kid down. He then informs Melio that he does not have a license for his weapon. Melio tells him not to worry, before coming out from behind the counter and beginning to batter the black kid (who may already be dead) with a length of metal piping. This is arguably the most gratuitous piece of violence in the entire film.

Argo (who died in 2004) was the kind of New York actor Scorsese relished working with: gruff, pugnacious, strong-featured. The working relationship between the two men started at the outset of their careers when Argo was cast as McIver in *Boxcar Bertha* (1972). He very occasionally played leads—for instance, his affecting turn as the gruff ex-cop with a terminal illness who falls under the influence of a young ingenue in Amos Kollek's *Queenie in Love* (2001)—but he was far better known as a character actor. Audiences who probably would not know him by name would recognize him instantly from his performances in more than 70 films and countless TV dramas. He worked with Jim Jarmusch, Abel Ferrara, and Woody Allen, as well as with Scorsese.

Often, Scorsese would also use performers whose lives mirrored those of the characters they were playing. This was certainly the case with Steven Prince, a fascinating and troubled individual who might easily have stumbled out of one of Scorsese's films. (Appropriately enough, Scorsese was later to make a documentary about Prince.) The two men had met through a mutual friend in 1968, when Scorsese was teaching film at New York University. At the time, Scorsese had been wearing a tie: not the kind of sartorial gesture to appeal to a counter-culture type like Prince. "I really gave him hell for that and that gave rise to our friendship," Prince recalled.

In subsequent years, Prince would work as a technical advisor, assistant, and even occasional bodyguard to Scorsese, as well as taking small parts in several of his films. The most memorable was as Easy Andy, the unctuous, smooth-talking gun salesman. Price was not a trained actor but he knew guns. "I grew up with firearms. We had a rifle range in the basement. My father was an arms expert and took me around the world on safaris. At 12 years old I trained for an hour with him every evening," he told *Positif* magazine. His dad collected guns and Steven followed in the family tradition. He calculated that the Prince household owned 352 pistols and 400 rifles.

Heroin addict, draft dodger, and one-time road manager for Neil Diamond, Prince had lived a colorful, beatnik life in the margins of American society. In *Taxi Driver*, with his corduroy jacket and shoulder-length hair, he looks strangely youthful, even innocent. He is—as Schrader's screenplay puts it—"an attractive young man." He is also ineffably sleazy. What makes his cameo so effective is its understated quality. He shows off his lethal merchandise to Travis in an anonymous hotel room overlooking the Hudson river without even asking what Travis wants the guns for. Once Travis takes the hook, he cannot stop himself from trying to sell him more gear. "How about some dope? Grass, hash, coke, mescaline?" he asks with all the effrontery of a mountebank hawking snake oil. Downers, uppers, crystal meth? When Travis spurns all these possibilities, he turns to cars. "I'll get you a brand new Cadillac with the pink slip for two grand."

Steven Prince provides a direct link between Scorsese and Quentin Tarantino, whose films *Reservoir Dogs* (1992) and *Pulp Fiction* (1994) carried Scorsese's fetish for violence to a new extreme. In *American Boy* (1978), Scorsese's documentary about him, Prince emerges as what one critic called "a blackly comic mirror image of Travis Bickle." In the documentary, Prince talks about injecting adrenaline into a companion who had overdosed. His story was clearly the inspiration for the famous scene in *Pulp Fiction* in which John Travolta's character Vincent plunges a syringe into the heart of the comatose and seemingly dead Mia (Uma Thurman).

American Boy is rarely seen today. Critics gave it a muted reception. Some were suspicious about the way Scorsese made Prince's story into the stuff of bar-room anecdote. "Prince is a soul steeped in self-deception, evading through uneasy laughter a self-loathing that seems to be eating away his frail shell of identity ... it's more than creepy to realize that Scorsese stole much of this for later film fiction and that he deliberately orchestrated this film into a 'theatrical' experience," wrote the *New Musical Express*.

Still, as his casting of Prince showed, Scorsese was a jackdaw: ready to draw on everything, however personal or seemingly off-limits, to strengthen his movies. The people he encountered and the experiences he had in his day-to-day life were the raw material that he would feed into his art.

the crew

To begin with: a massacre. Anyone with doubts about Scorsese's formal virtuosity or the brilliance of his collaborators behind the camera should watch the sequence at the end of *Taxi Driver* in which a mohawked Travis Bickle turns into an angel of vengeance. On a formal level, the sequence is stunning. Scorsese had been at New York University with Vietnam veteran Vic Magnotta (who plays a Secret Service photographer in *Taxi Driver*). Magnotta told him about the way certain US soldiers about to go on missions in the jungle in Vietnam would cut their hair mohawk-style in advance. "You knew that it was a special situation. People would give them wide berths. We thought it was a good idea [for Travis Bickle]," Scorsese noted. The mohawk style also reinforces the sense that this is an urban western.

Scorsese, his makeup artist Dick Smith, and cinematographer Michael Chapman went to extraordinary lengths to choreograph the carnage. "It may have seemed a wild sequence but it was extremely rehearsed," Jodie Foster, playing the 12-year-old prostitute Iris who is the catalyst behind Travis's rampage, later noted. The filmmakers had taken over a condemned building on 89th Street and Columbus Avenue. Here, they built Travis's apartment and the apartment used by Sport (Harvey Keitel) and his prostitutes.

"It was like going into an abattoir day after day," Chapman said of shooting on a location already drenched with movie blood. Dick Smith and his team built prosthetic limbs for

Travis to blow off, with dozens of cleverly concealed blood squibs primed to splash open from the stumps of severed arms or from Travis Bickle's injured neck. The hallway was so narrow that Smith could not simply hide out of frame as he might have done on other films. He therefore constructed bamboo poles with fishing lines to pull open the hidden bags of blood. He used mashed up bits of styrofoam cup and tiny pieces of sponge to represent the shards of skull and microscopic morsels of flesh blown away by Travis in his murderous rage. In order to carry out the elaborate, high-angle tracking shot in which the camera travels back through the scene of carnage left in Travis's wake, Chapman cut into the ceiling of the building and reinforced its foundations. "Otherwise, it would have fallen apart like a piece of cake."

On one level, this was Scorsese and Schrader's equivalent of the shoot-'em-up set-piece that almost every western ends with. It was also the most unsettling scene in a deeply unsettling film. The bleaching out of the original lurid reds that the National Ratings Board had demanded only served to make the sequence more morbid. The most exploitative horror films also often opted for the same dark, somber look. Scorsese, the artist, risked descending into the grimy underworld of such films as Tobe Hooper's *The Texas Chainsaw Massacre* (1974) or William Girdler's *Three on a Meathook* (1972), but his collaborators backed him all the way.

In turning 1970s New York into a dark, Babylonian city, "a hellscape worthy of Hieronymous Bosch" as one reviewer called it, Scorsese relied heavily on his resourceful and imaginative cinematographer, Michael Chapman. A Columbia graduate and sports nut who had "dropped out" to work as a freight brakeman on the Erie Lackawanna railroad before being drafted into the US army, Chapman was an unlikely recruit for the film business. He owed his start as a cameraman to his father-in-law, Joseph C. Brun, a French-born cinematographer whose credits ranged from *Flipper* (1963) to the Jayne Mansfield comedy *The Fat Spy* (1966). Brun managed to get Chapman into the Camera Guild and to help him find work as a focus puller and loader. His real break came when he was hired as camera operator on several films shot by ace cinematographer Gordon Willis, Alan J. Pakula's *Klute* (1971) and Francis Coppola's *The Godfather* (1972) and *The Godfather Part II* (1974) among them.

Chapman's first movie as cinematographer in his own right was Hal Ashby's *The Last Detail* (1973). Scripted by Robert Towne, this was a counterculture riposte to the Gene Kelly musical *On the Town* (1949). Jack Nicholson—looking suspiciously like one of the 1970s pop band The Village People—and Otis Young played sailors assigned to accompany young miscreant Randy Quaid across country to military prison. En route, they caroused, whored, and fought, and Nicholson became a surrogate father to ingenuous mother's boy Quaid. The film was picaresque and moving. Moreover, it boasted excellent location photography from Chapman that showed that the young cameraman was expert at shooting vérité-style on streets and trains.

Working on *Taxi Driver*, Chapman relished the chance to take a more expressionistic approach and to move away from the matter-of-fact, documentary style of *The Last Detail* (1973). "The project had enormous visual possibilities, and we felt it would be correct to be unusual and to do odd things with the camerawork and lighting," he told *American Cinematographer* magazine. "It would have been a terrible mistake to do any sort of surrealism in *The Last Detail*, but with *Taxi Driver*, the whole script was laden with visual information and suggestions and we went for it."

Goaded on by his director, Chapman used slow motion in an eerie and lyrical fashion. His shooting of neon-lit nighttime New York made the city seem both beautiful and menacing. Chapman and Scorsese were to push each other even farther with *Raging Bull* (1980), which Chapman (who won an Oscar nomination for his work) shot in black and white, but with sudden explosions of blood red.

In the shape of makeup artist Dick Smith, Scorsese had recruited another of the masters in his field. By all rights, Smith should not have been in the film business at all. A distant descendant of Ralph Waldo Emerson, Smith had studied medicine at Yale in the early 1940s. Makeup had become a hobby after he discovered a book revealing some of the secrets of the craft and had begun experimenting, turning friends into the Wolfman or Frankenstein's monster.

Smith is a necromancer of the makeup world, a greasepaint magician with an ability to change utterly an actor's appearance. His great skill is in aging actors. Smith did remarkable work on Marlon Brando for Francis Coppola's *The Godfather* (1972). Two layers of old-age stipple, some painted shadows and spots, and a denture device called a "plumper" to pad his jowls were all that was needed to transform Brando (who did not have the patience to sit around for hours) into the old patriarch, Don Corleone.

William Friedkin's *The Exorcist* (1973), another of his best-known credits, not only enabled him to "age" Max Von

Sydow from his mid-forties to his seventies to play Father Merrin, but also gave him plenty of scope to conjure up demons and contrive elaborate special-effects devices.

Arthur Penn's *Little Big Man* (1970) provided him with a novel challenge: transforming Dustin Hoffman into the oldest man alive, the 121-year-old Jack Crabb. Crabb's story, narrated in flashback in a croaky voice-over reminiscent of Grandpa Simpson, is so outrageously far-fetched that he is either—as the publicity material for the movie put it—"the most neglected hero in history or a liar of insane proportion." Smith's makeup helps give his tall tales at least the illusion of plausibility.

Smith won his Oscar for his work on F. Murray Abraham on Milos Forman's *Amadeus* (1984). His task, which he achieved with the usual élan, was to turn Abraham (playing Mozart's rival Salieri) from a sleek, conceited young court composer into an octogenarian, still consumed with bitterness.

Taxi Driver is not one of Smith's more prominent credits. In theory, a realistic, contemporary film with appropriately cast actors would not make heavy demands on his abilities to transform young into old or innocent teenagers into demons. However, the job of "special makeup" turned out to be a considerable challenge: he was in charge of the blood bags and of designing the wig that made audiences think Travis Bickle had a mohawk haircut for real.

Chapman and Smith's brilliance notwithstanding, the collaborator who really stood out on *Taxi Driver* (not least because the film was dedicated to him) was the composer, Bernard Herrmann. *Taxi Driver* boasts one of the most evocative music scores in all of Scorsese's movies. The opening is superb: the rain is pouring down; it's nighttime; as the yellow cab glides through the mist, there are martial rolls on the soundtrack, hinting at the violence lurking within the film. Then, as Scorsese cuts to a red-tinted close-up of the cab driver's eyes, we hear a jazzy saxophone theme, full of yearning and lyricism. There is something dreamy about the music, but we are immediately dragged back to the darkness at the core of the film by another roll of the drums. The music and the yellow cab go hand in hand. Whenever Travis is driving through nighttime New York, we hear the same ominous but lyrical theme. It is at its most insistent when Betsy is shown in slow motion, looking like a goddess as she walks through a sunlit street to her office, her beautifully coiffed hair billowing in the breeze, with Travis furtively watching her. We hear it again over the final sequences, as she boards Travis's cab again. Scorsese shows Travis gazing longingly at her in the mirror of the taxi cab. Again, her hair is blowing and she looks like the impossible object of desire.

Long before *Taxi Driver* began shooting, Scorsese had told producers Julia and Michael Phillips that the only composer he wanted for the film was Bernard Herrmann. Dutch director Wim Verstappen, best known for his controversial, taboo-breaking 1971 feature *Blue Movie*, had introduced Martin Scorsese to Herrmann, a 64-year-old film composer who happened to be living in London at the time.

Scorsese, De Palma, Schrader, and co. revered Herrmann, one of the legendary figures in Hollywood music history. The New York-born composer had an extraordinary filmography. He had written the scores for Orson Welles's *Citizen Kane* (1941) and *The Magnificent Ambersons* (1942).

Hitchcock, who admired him greatly, worked with him on *The Man Who Knew Too Much* (1935), *The Trouble with Harry* (1955), *Vertigo* (1958), *North by Northwest* (1959), *Psycho* (1960), and *Marnie* (1964). Truffaut hired him for *Fahrenheit 451* (1966) and *The Bride Wore Black* (1968). De Palma recruited him for his Hitchcock-influenced *Obsession* (1976), also scripted by Schrader.

Herrmann was a virtuoso. The son of Jewish immigrants, he had studied at Julliard and at New York University. He was a tough and rebarbative man. Hitchcock's biographer Donald Spoto notes that both Herrmann and Hitchcock "shared a dark, tragic sense of life, a brooding view of human relationships, and a compulsion to explore aesthetically the private world of the romantic fantasy."

For Herrmann, music was a fundamental part of filmmaking. He argued that without it, movies were lifeless and stilted. "All you'd have to do would be to look at any film without music and it would be almost unbearable to look at it," he once stated. Other composers credited him with moving film music away from a middle-European, symphonic sensibility and giving it a real vernacular American voice.

"Herrmann's music for *The Devil and Daniel Webster* [1941] had a great effect on my decision to become a film music composer," observed fellow composer Elmer Bernstein, who scored Scorsese's Edith Wharton adaptation, *The Age of Innocence* (1993), and *Bringing Out the Dead* (1999). "It [*The Devil*] was one of the earliest scores that had a peculiarly American voice. Herrmann fell back on a lot of folk music. If you think about who was writing film music in the United States in the 1940s, the names that spring to mind are Miklos Rozsa, Franz

Waxman, Max Steiner, Dimitri Tiomkin, all people who came from middle Europe ... along comes Bernard with a plaintive, less orchestrated American folk song idiom."

Herrmann may have been a pioneer, but collaborators had very mixed feelings about him. "Those who have worked with him know that he can be insulting, vehement, raucous, and even brutal," the *Saturday Review* noted in a 1968 profile. His obituarist in *Variety* likewise pointed out that he was "regarded as a tough person, hard to get along with, heartily disliked by many." *Taxi Driver* producer Julia Phillips called him "a disagreeable but talented old codger."

When Scorsese first broached the subject of his new film, the composer was typically brusque. "I don't do films about cab drivers," he told the young director. Nonetheless, Herrmann agreed to have lunch with him, read the script, and eventually signed on to score the movie.

At 64 years of age, Herrmann was in poor health. The composer had a heart condition. He probably should never have flown to the US to work on *Taxi Driver*, but was determined to finish what he must have known was going to be his last score. He struggled to come up with the main theme to *Taxi Driver*. Eventually, an assistant brought to his attention a piece of music he had written many years before and he adapted this for the movie.

The score was recorded in two days in late December 1975. Despite his health, Herrmann insisted on conducting the orchestra on the first day. The following evening, he died while resting in the Sheraton Hotel in Los Angeles. He was posthumously nominated for an Academy Award for his work on *Taxi Driver*. He was also nominated for his work on *Obsession*

(1976). In the event, he lost out to Jerry Goldsmith's score for *The Omen* (1976). *Taxi Driver* was dedicated to him. It was a fitting epitaph. Combining foreboding (the sound of jarring brass instruments, drum rolls, and snatches of harp music at moments of tension or danger) with an unlikely romanticism, it ranks alongside *Vertigo* (1958) and *Psycho* (1960) as one of his most immediately recognizable pieces of music.

There is a majesty to the score that often contrasts with the squalor of what is being depicted. This is at its most pronounced in that grim late sequence in which we see a bloodied Travis after the massacre and the high-angle camera then travels across the room, along the corridor, and down the stairs, revealing the carnage he has left in his wake. Herrmann combines slinky and melancholic jazz motifs with the full pomp of an orchestra. The result is both eerie and beguiling.

Herrmann was not the only musical influence on *Taxi Driver*, however. Another composer, Dave Blume, helped to music-direct the film. Scorsese later claimed he had designed the movie while listening to Van Morrison's dark, bluesy anthem 'TB Sheets'. The credits also feature a special thanks to Kris Kristofferson, the actor, country musician, and former Rhodes scholar. Kristofferson's music is not heard in the film, but his lyrics are quoted directly. In the scene in which Betsy meets Travis in a small New York coffee shop, she tells him he reminds her of the character described in a song by Kristofferson, "a prophet and a pusher, partly truth, partly fiction, a walking contradiction."

Travis, not noted for his sense of context or irony, is immensely offended by the idea that Betsy thinks he may be a pusher. (After all, his apocalyptic, final-reel mission is to kill all the pimps and pushers.) In fact, the lyrics come from a song called 'The Pilgrim: Chapter 33' that Kristofferson had written in 1971, not long after returning from shooting Dennis Hopper's ill-fated *The Last Movie* in Peru. The song is dedicated to a number of visionary characters with a wild, self-destructive streak, Hopper, Johnny Cash, and Ramblin' Jack Elliott among them. "See him wasted on the sidewalk in his jacket and his jeans / Wearin' yesterday's misfortunes like a smile" is how the song begins. Its description of someone "taking every wrong direction on his lonely way back home" cannot help but evoke an image of Travis alone in the big, bad city.

taxi driver's influences

Intriguingly, Travis Bickle had a real-life counterpart. The prototype for the antihero in *Taxi Driver* was a hapless would-be assassin and occasional diarist, Arthur Bremer, who tried several times in the early 1970s to kill President Nixon and eventually switched targets to Governor George Wallace, whom he shot and paralyzed in Maryland in May 1972. Footage still survives of the bungled assassination. The pro-segregation Wallace is greeting supporters when a gawky-looking man in a dark suit and dark glasses suddenly pops out of the crowd and shoots him from almost point-blank range.

There is pathos and a certain grim comedy in Bremer's story, which is worth retelling in detail, to highlight how closely it overlaps with the narrative of *Taxi Driver*. Bremer was the under-nerd, lonely, shunned at school, craving his 15 minutes of celebrity, even if he had to kill to get it. Born in Milwaukee in August 1950, he was the fourth of five children. His parents were heavy drinkers and his childhood was wretched. Arthur was a shy and reclusive boy, nicknamed "clown" at school because of the smile he wore well-nigh permanently in an attempt to ingratiate himself with a hostile world. His truck-driver father and his mother bickered endlessly. In one revealing school essay, he wrote that he liked to pretend he "was living with a television family and there was no one yelling at home and no one hit me."

Whatever miseries he endured, Bremer did not seem to his teachers to be an especially troubled child. He was far too timid to be a rebel. As a child, he was a churchgoer (mainly, it seemed, because it was a way of getting out of the house). During his adolescence, he became obsessed with pornography. He also began to stand up against his domineering mother, from whom he eventually became estranged altogether.

With no qualifications or ambitions, he floundered after he left school. He took English and photography courses, but dropped out of them. Bremer's paranoid tendencies first became apparent when he was in his early twenties. At the Milwaukee Athletic Club, where he worked as a waiter, customers complained that he talked to himself. To his fury and humiliation, his bosses demoted him, making him work in the kitchens instead. In late 1971, he took a job as a janitor in an elementary school. Here, he met and befriended a 15-year-old girl. On their first date, he showed her pornographic pictures and talked about sex to her. (This prefigures the bizarre scene in *Taxi Driver* in which Travis Bickle takes his date to a porno cinema.) Once she split up with him, Bremer reacted by shaving off all his hair to express his pain at his rejection. Chafing against the many slights the world inflicted on him, he bought two handguns. As he became ever more depressed and suicidal, he started reading widely about assassins in US history.

The reason we know so much about Bremer, who is still languishing in prison today, is that he kept a diary. Part of it was recovered from his car after the assassination attempt and published in 1973 as *An Assassin's Diary*. (The earlier part of the diary was found in freakish circumstances in 1980, when a construction worker named Sherman Griffin happened upon a cheap briefcase in a landfill refuse site.)

Bremer was swiftly put on trial for his attempted assassination of Wallace. The defense claimed that he was not guilty by reason of insanity. The prosecution argued that his planning showed a cunning and foresight that only a sane man was capable of. His lawyer's arguments that he was "a psychotic ... sick from the day he was born" fell on deaf ears. The jury found him guilty and the judge sentenced him to 63 years in Maryland State Penitentiary. His statement to the judge was pure Travis Bickle: "Well, Mr Marshall [the prosecutor] mentioned that he would like society to be protected from someone like me. Looking back on my life, I would have liked it if society had protected me from myself. That's all I have to say at this time."

Bremer had dreamed of a notoriety to rival that of Lee Harvey Oswald or John Wilkes Booth. In his fantasies, he thought not only of killing Nixon or Wallace, but also of dying a spectacular death himself. Instead, he was thrown into prison. A year later, *An Assassin's Diary* was published. It is a fascinating document, one that clearly had an influence on Schrader.

"I had read that he had done a diary, but I hadn't read the diary when I wrote the *Taxi Driver* script. Then, when the diary came out and I read it, I went 'Wow! That's quite similar,' Schrader says of the uncanny parallels between Bremer and Travis Bickle. "So I guess I was on the right track."

Bremer's spelling is atrocious. His diary entries in the six weeks leading up to the assassination attempt on Wallace range from half a page in length to nearly 20 pages. At times, his tone recalls that of Holden Caulfield in J.D. Salinger's *The Catcher in the Rye* (1951). There is a naivete and warped idealism about him. He frets about money, meticulously listing how much he is spending. There are asides about the music he has been listening to (Johnny Cash) and the latest film he saw (almost inevitably, it is Stanley Kubrick's *A Clockwork Orange*.) What is deeply unsettling is the matter-of-fact way he discusses his murder plans. There is a note of self-pity, too. He expects to die in his assassination attempt and presents the diary as a last testament.

Like Travis Bickle, Bremer tries to cope with his loneliness through voyeurism and pornography. In the entry for April 13th, 1972, he describes sitting in his hotel, watching "a beautiful naked lady" through binoculars. He also talks about how his nerve fails him when he tries to visit a massage parlor. Six days later, he steels himself and revisits the massage parlor. "A hairy character ... showed me a booklet of about 20 nude & near nude girls & said that 2 of them were working that day, a Sunday afternoon."

Bremer ends up with Alga, who tells him that she has a day job at an airline. She masturbates him, unsuccessfully trying to bring him to orgasm. He tries to grope her, but she tells him that is against the rules. All in all, it is an unsuccessful encounter. "Thought she didn't like me for my crew cut & straight cloths. She was dressed, somewhat like a hippie, when she was dressed," he confides to his diary. "I felt sorry for the kid. She was just like everybody else and she was only in it for the money."

The more you read Bremer's diaries, the more parallels emerge with *Taxi Driver*. Like Bremer, Travis Bickle is an assiduous chronicler of his own life. His narrative tone, verging from the nakedly confessional to the utterly banal, is also in keeping with that of Schrader's antihero. There is a comic interlude in which Bremer describes accidentally letting off one of his guns and then turning the television volume up to full blast so that his landlady does not notice. "I found a war movie on & if I wasn't fucking lucky, the Americans were giving the Japs everything they had."

In the same way that audiences are liable to identify with Travis Bickle because he is such a personable-seeming type of psychotic, readers cannot help but have a measure of sympathy for an assassin as inept and accident-prone as Arthur Bremer. Although he travels to Canada in an abortive attempt to kill Nixon, it quickly becomes apparent that he endorses Nixon's brand of conservatism and has no sympathy at all with the counterculture movement. "To be a rebel today you have to keep a job, wear a suit & stay apolitical. Now THAT'S REBELLION."

Bremer wants to be infamous, but acknowledges that killing Wallace will not be on a par with assassinating President Lincoln. "SHIT! I won't even rate a T.V. enteroption in Russia or Europe when the news breaks—they never heard of Wallace. I don't expect anybody to get a big thobbing erection from the news."

The diary entries end two days before he attempted to kill Wallace. A terse editor's note informs us that he was wearing sunglasses and a red, white, and blue shirt decorated with Wallace buttons as he lurked in the crowds, waiting for Wallace. After his arrest, the police searched his room in Milwaukee. They found a gun catalog, a confederate flag, and a pornographic comic book: just the sort of bric-a-brac they might have unearthed in Travis Bickle's New York apartment.

"It [the diary] was just about the little angry man who wants to be a somebody," Schrader reflects. The irony, he points out, is that "in our culture," if you go on a murderous spree or try to assassinate Governor Wallace, "you get to be a somebody."

After Bremer was safely behind bars, a would-be assassin called Sara Jane Moore took a shot at President Gerald Ford. To Schrader's amazement, she was put on the cover of *Newsweek* and achieved a fleeting celebrity. "I thought, wow, what a culture this is! You take a shot at the President and you're on the cover of the biggest news magazine."

Schrader's remarks are borne out by the extraordinary public and media interest in killers in the United States of the 1960s and 1970s. It seems astonishing now, but Lee Harvey Oswald was allowed to speak to the press in the days between the assassination of President Kennedy and his own killing at the hands of Jack Ruby in November 1963. There were many other assassins who became household names: Charles Whitman, the so-called "Texas Tower Sniper," who, in August 1966, hid at the top of the University of Texas tower in Austin and started taking potshots at passersby; Charles Starkweather and Caril Fugate, the delinquent teenage couple who went on a killing spree in the mid-1950s, indirectly inspiring such movies as Terrence Malick's *Badlands* (1973) and Oliver Stone's *Natural Born Killers* (1994); and the mass murderer Richard Speck.

Of course, Travis Bickle was much more than just a fictionalized version of Arthur Bremer or any other assassin.

Much of the character's richness and fascination lies in the welter of different influences that fed into his creation. Not that you would guess it by watching him skulk down Times Square or sit in porno theaters, but the antihero of *Taxi Driver* had a large number of literary antecedents. Schrader's screenplay for *Taxi Driver* opens with a quotation from novelist Thomas Wolfe: "The whole conviction of my life now rests upon the belief that loneliness, far from being a rare and curious phenomenon, is the central and inevitable fact of human existence." However close the identification he felt with Travis Bickle, Schrader could not disguise his high-culture roots. This was a man who had written a book on "transcendental style" in the films of Ozu, Bresson, and Dreyer, and who had been a Fellow of the American Film Institute at a very young age. Scorsese, too, was a literate and cultured figure with an encyclopedic knowledge of world cinema and experience in teaching film.

Part of the allure of *Taxi Driver* lies in the seamless way it combines two radically different approaches to storytelling. On the one hand, this is a lurid exploitation pic not so very far removed in subject matter from the vigilante thrillers of its era (for instance, Michael Winner's *Death Wish* films). Scorsese once described its style as "New York Gothic." On the other hand, even if they were exposing the sordid underbelly of 1970s New York and making nods to Corman-style B-movies as they did so, Schrader and Scorsese also had some very different influences in mind.

"I had read Dostoevsky's [1864 novella] *Notes from Underground* some years before and I had wanted to make a film of it; and *Taxi Driver* was the closest thing to it I'd come across," the director stated in *Scorsese on Scorsese*. Scan the opening of *Notes from Underground* and it quickly becomes apparent that the narrative voice is very close to that of Travis Bickle. "I am a sick man ... I am an angry man, I am an unattractive man," the protagonist of Dostoevsky's grim fable tells us.

Like Travis Bickle (or, indeed, Arthur Bremer), Dostoevsky's 40-year-old ex-civil-servant is an anonymous, disaffected "man of the crowd," who craves to be noticed. He also shares much of Bickle's self-loathing. "My debauches were solitary, nocturnal, secret, frightened, dirty, and full of a shame that did not leave me at the most abandoned moments ... I already carried the underground in my soul."

The narrator offers a tragicomic account of how he seeks redress after being barged out of the way by an officer in a tavern. He is desperate to fight a duel with the officer and thereby to avenge his wounded honor. The problem is that the officer has not yet noticed him. "I looked at him [the officer] with hatred and rage, and this went on ... for several years." He writes a letter to the officer that he is too scared to send. He tries to confront the officer in the park, but whenever he does so, he always stands aside and cedes way to the officer at the last moment. He tries to pick quarrels with old school friends. He has an encounter with a 20-year-old prostitute, whom he mocks and humiliates, as if doing so might help exorcise his own miseries. When Pauline Kael (then the most influential critic in the US) reviewed *Taxi Driver* in *The New Yorker* in February 1976, her piece was headlined "Underground Man."

If the links with Dostoevsky's novella are self-evident, so is Schrader's debt to Sartre's *Nausea*. When he had just been discharged from hospital and was convalescing from a gastric ulcer, the screenwriter re-read Sartre's novel and Albert Camus's *L'Etranger*. "I saw them as a philosophical wellspring of this kind of underground character."

Sartre's narrator is a troubled young writer called Antoine Roquentin. Like Travis Bickle, he claims that he is recently returned from Southeast Asia. "I can't understand why I was in Indo-China. What was I doing there?" Antoine asks early in the novel. Back home in provincial France, he is in limbo: tortured by the metaphysical meaninglessness of existence. He is obsessed by banal details of his everyday life: the shape of an ink bottle, the feel of a door handle, the significance of bits of paper he finds discarded in the street.

Scorsese, too, fetishizes the smallest objects and incidents in Travis Bickle's world: witness his extreme close-up of an Alka-Seltzer tablet dissolving in a glass of water (an idea pinched from Jean-Luc Godard's *Two Or Three Things I Know About Her* (1966) or the sordid scene showing him wipe down the back seat of his taxi cab as his voice-over recounts how he has to clean "the come" and "the blood" left by his passengers. There are constant shots of Bickle's eyes, emphasizing both his voyeurism and the fact that (in Schrader's original screenplay at least) everything is seen entirely from his perspective.

In his milder moments, Travis's voice carries echoes of Holden Caulfield, the sulky but idealistic antihero of J.D. Salinger's superb 1951 novel *The Catcher In The Rye*. This, too, was a story about a young loner adrift on the streets of New

York. Holden's confessional, first-person narrative style, gauche, spiky, and lyrical by turns, is not so far removed from Travis's voice-overs.

Leaf through the book and you will find the same mix of defiance and perversity in Holden as in Scorsese's cab driver. "Boy, I couldn't get off that goddam Broadway fast enough," Holden expresses his disgust at the movie-going crowds. "In case you don't live in New York, the Wicker Bar is in this sort of swanky hotel, the Seton Hotel ... it's one of those places that are supposed to be very sophisticated and all, and the phonies are coming out of the windows," he tells us at the start of one chapter. "Every time I came to the end of a block and stepped off the goddamed kerb, I had this feeling that I'd never get to the other side of the street. I thought I'd just go down, down, down, and nobody'd ever see me again," he confides his nightmarish vision late in the novel.

For Schrader, the influence of Bresson's 1959 feature *Pickpocket* was impossible to shrug off. "An unmitigated masterpiece," he called it. "I adore *Pickpocket* and can watch it endlessly. To me, it's as close to perfect as there can be."

Inspired by Dostoevsky's *Crime and Punishment* (1866), *Pickpocket* is the story of a loner adrift on the streets of Paris. Michel (Martin La Salle) becomes a petty thief. For him, stealing is a vocation. He is both craftsman and artist. With his long, slender fingers, he is extraordinarily adept at plucking wallets out of pockets or even sliding off victims' watches. There is a telling scene early in the movie in which he holds forth on his theories about his chosen life. "Can we not admit that certain skilled men, gifted with intelligence, talent, or even genius, and so indispensable to society, rather than stagnate, should be free to disobey laws in certain cases?" Like Travis Bickle, the pickpocket has the sense that he is a superman, somehow exempt from the rules of society.

Intriguingly, *Pickpocket* uses the same voice-over narration as *Taxi Driver*. The two films have many themes in common. The pickpocket, we know, is afflicted by the same searing loneliness that afflicts Travis. Just as Travis practices again and again in front of a mirror pulling guns from holsters, the pickpocket teaches himself how to pluck away watches and purses. He is bright and resourceful, but cannot escape his compulsion to steal. Unlike *Taxi Driver*, *Pickpocket* is a redemptive tale. The pickpocket may end up behind bars, but at least he finds the woman he loves. Travis, by contrast, is far too unstable a personality to be able to build or sustain a relationship.

Scorsese shared Schrader's passion for Bresson, but in interviews, *Pickpocket* was not the first Bresson movie he cited. For him, Bresson's 1950 feature, *Diary of a Country Priest*, was more the point of reference. Although set in an environment utterly different from that of *Taxi Driver*, namely the French countryside, it boasts a protagonist almost as mixed up as Travis himself. The priest (Claude Laydu) is a young, intensely spiritual man, ministering to a congregation of coarse peasants. He is sickly, effete, and struggles to establish any kind of rapport with the locals, yet Bresson shows him in an idealized light. He has dedication and is prepared to suffer, even to die, for it. The film deals with faith and spirituality in an unflinching way. Travis is like a distorted parody of the priest, but he too suffers stomach ailments and he too is an isolated, lonely man, unable to connect with the society around him.

Whether or not Travis is an existential loner in the philosophical sense described by Sartre, he is definitely the quintessential American "underground man."

The writer and the director of *Taxi Driver* each combined the roles of hustler and artist. They both had very healthy egos and were hugely ambitious. They wanted to shock and outrage audiences and to serve up a denouement as bloody as that found in Sam Peckinpah's *The Wild Bunch* (1969). They had serious points to make about gun culture and political corruption in the United States of the 1970s, in the wake of Watergate and the Vietnam War. They paid lip service to the myth of the self-destructive poet. Scorsese used to say that he could not envisage living beyond the age of 40. With their machismo and bravado, they sounded almost like cowboys.

It is a long way from the gaudy, neon-lit 1970s Times Square, with its clip joints, massage parlors, and porno theaters, to the rugged, wholesome terrain of the Hollywood western. Nonetheless, the spirit of John Ford and Sam Peckinpah hovers over *Taxi Driver*. Scorsese and Schrader had little interest in the child-like, simple-minded morality of the early days of the western. Their fascination is with the dark and obsessive undercurrents found in works like Ford's *The Searchers* (1956) or Anthony Mann's films with James Stewart, such as *The Naked Spur* (1953) and *The Man From Laramie* (1955), in which violence and revenge are in the foreground.

The blood-saturated final-reel shootout of *Taxi Driver* was directly inspired by the extraordinary scenes at the end of Peckinpah's *The Wild Bunch* (1969). In a symphony of slow-motion violence, the aging cowboys led by William Holden stage a suicidal shootout with the soldiers of General

Malpache's Mexican army to revenge the torture and killing of one of their comrades. Malpache slits Angel's throat in front of them. That is the cue for battle. The bloodletting defies any narrative logic. Peckinpah wallows in the killing. There is a famous shot of Warren Oates, with bullet wounds all over him, holding the machine gun and blasting soldier after soldier to oblivion. Women are killed. Holden's character is shot by a little boy. In the end, we are left with an apocalyptic sequence that might have been culled from a Renaissance painting of the day of judgment. Walls are smeared with blood. The ground is littered with corpses that the bounty hunters cheerily loot. "You're in a world of glorified bloodshed," Schrader noted of the sequence. "These four men were entering into psychopath's heaven."

Scorsese's achievement in *Taxi Driver* is to give a sequence set in a cramped downtown New York brothel the same intensity found in Peckinpah's famous final-reel bloodbath. Schrader called it "the psychopath's second coming." The director did not even attempt to deny that this was the sequence he relished most of all. "I like the idea of spurting blood," he admitted. "It reminds me ... God, it reminds me ... it's like a purification ... you know the fountains of blood ... but it's realistic, too. The guy that puts the blood ... I said give me a little more, he said that is going to be a lot, I said that's OK."

In westerns, the violence is at a remove. We know that what we are watching happened safely in the past and that the codes of behavior that applied in the lawless frontier lands have long since changed. There is a selfconsciously mythic undertow to *The Wild Bunch* (1969). The whole film is about the last stand of a group of old-timers who cannot adapt to changing ways. Although some critics dubbed the massacre sequence pornographic, it is also fitting that these men who have grown up amid violence should be consumed by violence. They were never going to grow old gracefully and Peckinpah was determined to give them the most spectacular send-off imaginable.

No such arguments can be made about Travis Bickle's shootout with the pimps in a cramped apartment block in contemporary New York's Lower East Side. This is happening in the here and now, in a long, narrow hallway. It is vigilante violence and it is appalling to watch. In the screenplay, Schrader's instructions are explicit. He dryly writes that an old man's right hand "has been blown off at the forearm"; that a bullet has ripped through the left of Travis's neck; that Travis fills a private cop's face "full of bullet holes"; that the old man's "palm is impaled on a knife." Scorsese's storyboard drawings of the sequence were equally explicit. His cartoon sketches show stick insects with bullets exploding through their chests.

Travis Bickle's quest to save the 12-year-old prostitute from her life among the pimps and lowlifes also has clear parallels with Ford's *The Searchers* (1956). In Ford's western, Ethan Edwards (John Wayne) is searching for his niece (Natalie Wood), who was kidnapped and raised by Indians after the slaughter of her parents. Edwards is very different from Travis Bickle. He is a stern, slow-moving, old patriarch whose bitterness is self-evident. What he shares with Travis is an utter loathing for the people who have stolen away (and corrupted) an innocent young girl.

Throughout *Taxi Driver*, we hear Travis making often overtly racist remarks about the "scum on the sidewalk." Ethan Edwards' remarks about the Comanches are every bit as virulent and aggressive.

In a scene that still shocks audiences more accustomed to seeing John Wayne as an upstanding all-American hero, he shoots at the corpse of a dead Indian. When asked why, he explains that in Comanche culture, someone "who ain't got no eyes is condemned to wander the spirit land—he has to wander forever between the winds."

The irony is that Ethan himself is the man who does not seem to belong anywhere. Like Travis, he has cut his roots with family and background. When finally he tracks down his niece, we suspect that he is going to kill her because she has been living for so long as a Comanche herself. Instead, in probably the most affecting scene in all of Ford's work, he tells her it is time "to go home." For just an instance, he is able to rise above his own prejudices.

Schrader and Scorsese allow Travis Bickle no such moment of grace. What they do offer him is the brief celebrity he so craves. "You can work for 40 years to find a cure for cancer and never be acknowledged, but take a shot at the president and you're a hero," Schrader later joked of the way that vigilantes and assassins are invariably given a spot in the limelight at the expense of humanitarians.

Two years after *Taxi Driver*, Schrader again paid hommage to *The Searchers* (1956) in his film *Hardcore* (1978), in which a young girl is likewise abducted. In this case, she is whisked away from a Calvinist convention, kidnapped by a snuff movie producer who sets her to work on porno films. Her father (George C. Scott) is the Ethan Edwards type, trying to rescue her and restore her to family life.

Robert De Niro was later to appear in Michael Cimino's *The Deer Hunter* (1978). He gives another exemplary performance as Michael, the Pennsylvania steelworker sent to Vietnam. True, Michael sometimes behaves like an action-movie hero. The moment midway through a game of Russian roulette when he turns the gun on his sadistic captors and frees his two friends would not look out of place in a *Rambo* movie. However, De Niro is far too subtle an actor simply to play the *Boy's Own* hero. His character is the antithesis of Travis Bickle. De Niro conveys brilliantly Michael's innate resourcefulness and dignity, as well as his growing anguish at the fate of his friends. As ever, De Niro prepared assiduously for his role, meeting and spending time with steelworkers (few of whom recognized him) over the course of several weeks. His muted performance was perfectly complemented by Vilmos Szigmond's rich, dark cinematography.

Taxi Driver may not be a gangster movie, but this is a genre Scorsese knows inside out and draws heavily on. In his influential 1940s essay "The Gangster as Tragic Hero," critic Robert Warshow explored the way in which gangster films challenged and undermined the upbeat optimism to which the United States "as a social and political organization" was committed. "The gangster," Warshow wrote, "is the man of the city, with the city's language and knowledge, with its queer and dishonest skills." Warshow evoked an image of the gangster at the heart of a twilight urban world in which fatalism and violence rule. This is precisely the world that Travis Bickle inhabits.

Taxi Driver shares many of the hallmarks of classic film noir. The use of voice-over is a leitmotif of the genre, whether in Billy Wilder's *Double Indemnity* (1944) or Abraham Polonsky's *Force of Evil* (1948). The jazzy, mournful Bernard Herrmann music and the nighttime scenes of New York, in which we see Travis's yellow cab emerging through the mist or gliding past the neon-lit bars and porno theaters, are likewise recognizable from the elegiac Hollywood gangster films of the 1940s and 1950s. Scorsese cited Irving Lerner's low-budget 1958 noir, *Murder by Contract*, about a contract killer, as a direct influence on *Taxi Driver*. "Above all, it gave us an inside look into the mind of a man who kills for a living, and it was pretty frightening," he observed.

Scorsese loved gangster films. Whether it was the psychopathic behavior of James Cagney, squashing a grapefruit in his girlfriend's face in *The Public Enemy* (1931), or Paul Muni letting rip with a machine gun in *Scarface* (1932), he had seen and studied all the key pictures in the genre. He was also a fan of the lurid, pulpy style of Sam Fuller, one of the few US directors whose movies are regularly peopled by characters even more unhinged than Travis Bickle. In films like *Shock Corridor* (1963), *The Naked Kiss* (1965), and *White Dog* (1982), Fuller tackles such subjects as racism, paedophilia, and prostitution without blinking. His filmmaking took its cue from his background as a crime reporter writing for mass-market newspapers. "He [Fuller] has a tabloid mentality ... he has to hit you with the headlines, hit you with the prose," Scorsese noted admiringly even as he set about emulating the old master.

The best-known images from Fuller movies are often lurid

and overstated, but they are also very powerful. Take, for example, Constance Towers as the prostitute throwing off her wig and beating up her pimp at the start of *The Naked Kiss*, or the scenes of the flooded lunatic asylum in *Shock Corridor*. Early on in his newspaper career, Fuller learned a key lesson from his mentor Arthur Brisbane (William Randolph Hearst's editor-in-chief): "To get truth is very difficult unless you are personally involved." As a filmmaker, Scorsese was always personally involved.

When it came to his own movies, Scorsese borrowed Fuller's device of using tracking shots when he was showing violence. "Doing that one long take creates so much in emotional impact, giving you a sense of being swept up in the fury and the anger, that you begin to understand more why it is happening," he told David Thompson and Ian Christie in *Scorsese on Scorsese*. "What Sam always says is that emotional violence is much more terrifying than physical violence."

In *Park Row* (1952), Fuller's film about the newspaper business, there is a famous tracking shot showing the sheer chaos and violence when a newspaper circulation war breaks out. Scorsese drew on this directly when he was making *Mean Streets* (1973). The famous tracking shot at the end of *Taxi Driver*, when Travis has just killed the pimps, had a hint of Fuller about it, too.

Fuller not only influenced the way Scorsese made films, but he also changed the way the Italian-American director talked about them. There is a tradition of machismo and bravado in filmmakers' discourse stretching back to the time when silent film pioneer D.W. Griffith said that "all you need to make a movie is a girl and a gun." Fuller knew how to speak up his movies better than anyone. Smoking his trademark cigar, he would snarl out remarks like "Heroes? Don't believe in them," or "If the first scene doesn't give you a hard-on, throw the whole thing away."

Scorsese was almost equally colorful in his language at the time *Taxi Driver* was released. Yes, he told journalists, the film had strong autobiographical elements. "It's true ... I spatter bits of myself all over the screen. I've got to admit that all of my films, with the exception of *Boxcar Bertha* [1972] which was hack work for Corman, are in some sense autobiographical in that they draw on my own experience. I go to shrinks. But they might as well look at the movies."

Another obvious source of inspiration for Scorsese when it came to showing imagery of the city in its goriest, most squalid guises was the work of the celebrated crime photographer Arthur "Weegee" Fellig. No one could be more matter of fact about covering the dark side of New York City nightlife than Weegee. "The easiest kind of job to cover was a murder," the photographer claimed. "The stiff would be laying on the ground and so he couldn't get up and walk away." He also had precisely the same curiosity about every aspect of New York life as Scorsese. Couples kissing in coffee shops, drunkards adrift in the streets, chorus girls in G-strings, kids blowing bubblegum while watching a movie, cops covering up the body of a murder victim with newspapers and coats, New Yorkers jam-packed on the beach, sweltering in the heat on Coney Island: Weegee would cover it all. He would also make sure he had the details correct, so he could caption the pictures. He lived across the road from police headquarters. Just like Travis Bickle, he prowled through nighttime New York. Just like Scorsese, he knew Manhattan's Lower East Side intimately.

A European film that matched *Taxi Driver* in terms of intensity and lurid violence was Jean-Luc Godard's satire *Weekend* (1967). By coincidence, Scorsese was in Paris in 1968 at the time of the student riots provoked by the De Gaulle government's decision to sack Henri Langlois as curator of the Cinémathèque. *Weekend* features car crashes, casual shootings, and even scenes of cannibalism. As Raoul Coutard, Godard's cinematographer, later admitted, the maverick director's prime aim in making *Weekend* was to "annoy the hell out of his producer." He was also set on pushing back boundaries of film language (witness his jump cuts, his hugely elaborate tracking shots, his use of voice-over and intertitles). This was the height of the Vietnam War. Magazines, newspapers, and TV programs were full of images of violence, albeit at a safe remove, many thousands of miles away. Godard's trick was to bring that violence into the everyday world of a pampered, bourgeois couple. In *Taxi Driver*, Scorsese does something similar, showing how the trauma of the Vietnam War was spilling over into ordinary civilian life.

As Paul Schrader's brother, Leonard Schrader, shows in his documentary *The Killing of America* (1980), something very strange and disturbing was happening in the US at the time that *Taxi Driver* was made. Homicide statistics had risen in an alarming and seemingly inexplicable way. Between 1900 and 1963, the relative murder rate in the US hardly changed at all, despite the easy availability of guns. After 1963, the rates rocketed. "If you look at the statistics, it's pretty clear the assassination of Kennedy radically changed murder in

America," Leonard Schrader claimed. For whatever reason, murder became a kind of fad, "a new form of self-therapy—Americans using other Americans in life or death situations to work out their problems," as Schrader put it. By 1970, there were over 100 million guns in the country: around two for every household.

One of the most disturbing and unsettling scenes in *Taxi Driver* comes when Travis Bickle buys his weaponry. He is like a kid let loose in a candy store. Andy, the gun salesman (played in oily, reptilian fashion by Steven Prince), plays on his fascination, tantalizing him with ever more graphic descriptions of what the guns can do. There is the .44 Magnum: "A monster, can stop a car: put a bullet right into the block." There is the .38 Smith and Wesson Special: "That'll stop anything that moves and it's handy, flexible." There is the .32 revolver and the Colt .25, "a fine little gun." Travis, who has been saving up all his money from those draining, all-night-long double shifts in his cab, buys the lot.

The 1970s was the decade when vigilante movies topped box-office charts. Don Siegel's *Dirty Harry* (1971), with Clint Eastwood as .44 Magnum-wielding Harry Callahan, was the first in a wave of films celebrating the murderous antics of rogue cops, bounty hunters, and vengeful husbands, doing their bit to keep the streets of the United States clean for its citizens. "A specious, phony glorification of police and criminal brutality ... Clint Eastwood is a superhero whose antics become almost satire," noted *Variety* in a disapproving review.

It is easy to "read" *Dirty Harry* and its imitators (notably Michael Winner's *Death Wish* films) in sociological terms, as evidence of a malaise in white middle-class America. These were times of enormous social and political turbulence. The growth in gun crime, the rise in unemployment, the blow to self-esteem caused by reverses in Vietnam, the counterculture, black power, and feminism all served to undermine self-confidence. On a symbolic level, Eastwood and Charles Bronson were restoring the old, conservative order, albeit at the end of a gun barrel.

There were striking parallels between John Milius, who scripted *Dirty Harry* as well as films such as rugged *Boys' Own* stories *Jeremiah Johnson* (1972) and *The Wind and the Lion* (1975), and Schrader. They were both seemingly enthralled by the hoary old myth of the womanizing, hard-living, hard-drinking male writer—Dirty Harry with a typewriter instead of a .44 Magnum. Milius was already successful by the time Schrader met him in the early 1970s, but the two writers gravitated toward one another. In Peter Biskind's book, *Easy Riders, Raging Bulls*, producer Howard Rosenman notes that Schrader was fascinated by "that male energy, Hemingway-esque thing of Milius's, as well as that self-destructive, killing himself, writer thing." Another of Biskind's sources, writer and actor L.M. Kit Carson, noted that "Schrader was in love with Milius, no two ways about it. He imitated Milius's behavior, the idea being, if you acted crazy, it scared people and they would respect you."

Midway through *Taxi Driver*, Travis decides to get himself in shape. He quits smoking and begins an arduous regime of exercise. "Total organization is necessary. Every muscle must be right," he writes in his diary as he is shown doing sit-ups and press-ups, holding his arm unflinching in a flame and practising his sharp shooting. These scenes anticipate Schrader's later film, *Mishima* (1985), a stylized biopic of the Japanese writer who likewise had a Charles Atlas-like fascination with his own body. In the course of that film, Mishima transforms himself from a weedy, bookish type who might have had sand kicked in his eye on the beach into a latterday samurai warrior. He even raises his own private army and, just like Travis, Mishima has suicidal fantasies of going out in a blaze of glory.

"Schrader ... seems plainly (and quite unashamedly) neo-Fascist: his films (as writer and director) amount to a systematic repudiation of all minority groups and any possible social alternative, in order to re-assert a quasi-mythical sense of male supremacy, heterosexual superiority, and a totally spurious 'transcendence' (which amounts to little more than one person's right to slaughter other people, on the basis of some supposed achievement of spiritual transfiguration, with no foundation in material reality)," complained influential critic Robin Wood.

There is one vital aspect of *Taxi Driver* that Wood risks overlooking: its sense of irony. Schrader and Scorsese never attempt to disguise Travis's shortcomings. Even in his vocation as assassin, he is a lamentable failure. Just as Arthur Bremer downsized his ambition and switched targets from the inaccessible, closely guarded President Nixon to Governor Wallace, Travis abandons his plans to shoot presidential hopeful Charles Palantine, and settles for a few low-life pimps instead.

Taxi Driver does not gild its central character. It is self-evident that Travis is a psychopath with racist leanings and a disastrous lack of social skills. There is nothing remotely coherent about his philosophy of life. He is an avid consumer of pornography who sets himself a moral mission to save a 12-year-old prostitute from a life of depravity. He wants to gun down Palantine even though the politician (it is implied) shares his own desires to clean "the scum, the filth" off the sidewalks. If he is a modern, urban equivalent to the Nietzschean superman, he is one with very ragged edges. Scorsese's trick, helped immeasurably by Robert De Niro's charismatic and occasionally tongue-in-cheek performance, is to make a character with so many deeply obnoxious traits partly sympathetic. One of the deepest ironies about the ending of the film is that he becomes a kind of folk hero, written about by the press ("Taxi-Driver Hero!") in absurdly glowing terms and thanked profusely as he recuperates in hospital by the prostitute's parents. The audience knows that he is a deeply disturbed individual who has not been cured of his illness. Like the evil spirits and long-taloned ghouls in Hollywood horror films, we guess that he might strike again.

Some critics have likened Travis in his massacre gear to the verminous, bloodsucking protagonist played by Max Schreck in the classic German silent horror movie *Nosferatu* (1922). Another even more apt comparison might be with the work of Edgar Allan Poe. In particular, there is a story by Poe called *The Man of the Crowd* in which the narrator, recently recovered from a long illness, sits in a crowded London coffee house and looks out through the "smokey panes" at the tides of humanity rolling by. The narrator regards these passersby with the same mix of distaste and anthropological curiosity that Travis Bickle shows as he watches the flotsam and jetsam of New York nightlife from his cab booth. "All the animals come out at night: whores, skunk pussies, buggers, queens, fairies, dopers, junkies, sick, venal," Travis murmurs in the voice-over that opens *Taxi Driver*.

From his eyrie, Poe's unnamed narrator notes the "tribes of clerks," the "jostlers," the "men of leisure," the "swell pickpockets," the "gamblers" and "sharpers," the "Jew pedlars," the "professional street beggars," the "feeble and ghastly invalids," and the drunkards. There is even a description of a child prostitute, "the mere child of immature form, yet, from long association, an adept in the dreadful coquetries of her trade, and burning with a rabid ambition to be ranked the equal of her elders in vice."

Among this crowd, the narrator spots a face that fascinates him: that of "the man of the crowd." There is something horrifying but also fascinating about this man, with his features that denote avarice, malice, triumph, and despair. It is as if this man embodies all the contradictory emotions of those swirling around him.

It may be fanciful to regard Poe's "man of the crowd" as a 19th-century ancestor of Travis Bickle, but there are self-evident links between Poe's *Tales of Mystery and Imagination* and the work of Martin Scorsese. The director even described his film as "a cross between Gothic horror and *The New York Daily News*." One of his early mentors (for whom he made 1972's *Boxcar Bertha*) was the cult horror film director Roger Corman, renowned for his Poe adaptations. This was confirmed in *Mean Streets* (1973), which he shot with the same Corman crew who had worked on *Boxcar Bertha*, and in which Scorsese had included a clip from Corman's *Tomb of Ligeia* (1965) by way of homage.

Corman's Poe adaptations were characterized by their Baroque production design and lush color cinematography. In certain of the more stylized sequences of *Taxi Driver*, for instance Travis's yellow cab appearing in slow motion out of the nighttime mist or the expressionistic use of the color red in the final sequence, Scorsese and his cinematographer Michael Chapman seem to be paying sly tribute to Corman's eerie, morbid costume melodramas.

Another horror film that was an important formative influence on Scorsese was Michael Powell's *Peeping Tom* (1960). This, too, was a movie about an obsessive loner. Mark Lewis (Carl Boehm) is a milk-drinking, dufflecoat wearing psychopath who stabs women with the dagger in the leg of his camera tripod while always trying to capture the precise moment of their death on film. He has several traits in common with Travis Bickle. He, too, is awkward with women. He shares Travis's naivete. With both men, there is a sense that they are little boys lost in the big, bad city. Travis and Mark are ardent voyeurs. As Powell and Scorsese both attest, voyeurism is at the root of the moviegoing experience.

"I remember [cinematographer] Michael Chapman, who shot *Taxi Driver* and *Raging Bull* [1980] for me, was watching *Peeping Tom* on television one night and he phoned me about one line in the film: 'All this filming is not healthy.' He was laughing because it reminded him of me," Scorsese noted in *Scorsese on Scorsese*.

The Italian-American director was equally enthusiastic about the work of B-horror movie meister Jacques Tourneur, especially his 1942 feature *Cat People*. What he relished was the way in which Tourneur used the horror genre to confront the hidden, psychological anxieties of his characters, whether it be their fears about sexuality, their terror of death, or their own physical cowardice.

"After Tourneur opened Pandora's box, things were never the same," Scorsese noted. "It may have gone unnoticed at first, but a strange darkness crept into American films. A feeling of insecurity, disorientation, and foreboding, as though the ground could safely give way under your feet."

getting the film made

For the 33-year-old Martin Scorsese, *Taxi Driver* was a "labor of love." He had long been lobbying to be allowed to direct the film. He first read Paul Schrader's script in the early 1970s and immediately warmed to its apocalyptic evocation of the New York of the era. "When I read the script, I felt it was a film I had to make," he admitted.

Even to get a whiff of the job, Scorsese needed to lobby relentlessly. He began gatecrashing parties, trying to buttonhole Schrader and *Taxi Driver*'s 30-year-old producer, Julia Phillips. His problem was that he had no track record. The only features he had to his credit were *Who's That Knocking at My Door* (1968), a bravura effort but one with the hallmarks of a glorified student film, and *Boxcar Bertha* (1972), a low-budget, Bonnie and Clyde-style exploitation picture made under the aegis of Roger Corman, "King of the B's."

Schrader did not think much of the diminutive Italian-American director, to whom he was introduced by their mutual friend Brian De Palma. Nor did Julia Phillips. "Marty sidles up to me at parties and tells me in his intense undertone how much he wants to do this picture," she later recalled. "He is shoulder high and sometimes I find myself talking out of the side of my mouth into the top of his hair. Not a chance. Forget it. Come back when you've done something besides *Boxcar Bertha*."

Scorsese had never been first in mind for *Taxi Driver*. De Palma had expressed an interest in directing. There was vague talk of Robert Mulligan, an ex-theology student and son of a New York policeman whose only real film of note was *To Kill a Mocking Bird* (1962), taking on the directing duties. Other names were also considered, John Milius, Irving Kershner, and Lamont Johnson among them. By 1975, though, the Italian-American had finally earned his spurs. With *Mean Streets* (1973), his blistering account of petty hoodlums adrift in New York's Little Italy, Scorsese had proved he was a filmmaker with a personal vision and the ability to elicit ferociously intense performances. With *Alice Doesn't Live Here Anymore* (1974), his Oscar-winning weepie about a widow on the road trying to make a living as a singer, he showed he could handle populist, mainstream material worlds away from the machismo of the gangster genre.

Not only was Scorsese on the up and up, but Robert De Niro was also so impressive as Johnny Boy, the delinquent, livewire antihero of *Mean Streets*, that Francis Coppola cast him in *The Godfather Part II* (1974), for which he won an Oscar. Schrader, too, was in demand. The former film critic turned scriptwriter had sold his screenplay for *The Yakuza* (1975) to Warner Bros for $350,000.

"Julia [Phillips] and I went to a rough cut of *Mean Streets* and walked out and said it [*Taxi Driver*] has got to be done with Bob [De Niro] and Marty [Scorsese]," Schrader recalled. There was a hitch: Scorsese wanted Harvey Keitel for the leading role. "He knew Harvey, he didn't know Bob that well at the time," Schrader noted. To complicate matters further,

Tony Bill (Julia and Michael Phillips's producing partner) was keen to cast Jeff Bridges in the lead role. This was not a notion that appealed to Schrader. "I thought that the movie wouldn't work. Jeff is a good actor, but he is not that actor." Schrader's opposition to Bridges drove a wedge between the Phillipses and Tony Bill (who had once lobbied for Al Pacino to play Travis Bickle). It soon became clear precisely who the key players were going to be: Schrader, Scorsese, and De Niro, with the Phillips as producers.

In theory, this was still a project that any studio would want to bankroll: husband and wife Julia and Michael Phillips were the most successful young producers in Hollywood. Scorsese was so coveted that another rising young producer, Irwin Winkler, had already sounded him out about directing the epic 1940s-set musical *New York, New York*. De Niro was the new golden boy and everyone acknowledged Schrader as an A-list writer.

It is a measure of how uncomfortable Hollywood was with *Taxi Driver* that even with this "dream team," the purse strings were slow to loosen. Studio bosses were openly discomfited by Schrader's strange, morbid morality tale about a 26-year-old New York cab driver called Travis Bickle. The beautifully written screenplay did nothing to allay their fears about the nihilism, cynicism, and violence of the material.

"He [Bickle] seems to have wandered in from a land where it is always cold, a country where the inhabitants seldom speak. The head moves, the expression changes, but the eyes remain ever-fixed, unblinking, piercing empty space," Schrader writes in his opening paragraph. It is strong, evocative stuff—if you are a novelist trying to describe an existential loner. For would-be financiers and producers, the impression is less seductive. Who wants to see movies about consummate loners? Where were the merchandizing possibilities in a movie about a psychopathic cab driver? This was the summer of *Jaws*, Steven Spielberg's tall tale about a great white shark that helped usher in the era of the "summer tentpole movie." As Carl Gottlieb, who scripted *Jaws*, later pointed out, the film "established a business model and release pattern for large-scale summer movies that persists to this day." It also won three Oscars and quickly became the highest grossing film of its time.

Maybe if Schrader had written about killer crocodiles or swarms of deadly bees, Hollywood might have been more accommodating. However, a miasmatic cloud hung over Travis Bickle. Julia Phillips and her husband Michael had optioned the screenplay, but even she did not seem to like it much. "I had found nothing attractive about *Taxi Driver* when I first read it, except for its sociology," she later confessed. "Travis was a nut case, a valid nut case but a nut case. I thought Schrader was, too." Schrader recalls the screenplay bouncing around from studio to studio. The response was always the same. "People said wow, that's a good script, somebody should make it … but not us."

Besides, studio bosses always looked at the bottom line. *Alice Doesn't Live Here Anymore* (1974) had made money, but *Mean Streets* (1973), despite the rhapsodic reviews, had not. Audiences clearly found it too disturbing. There was little possibility—or so the studios reasoned—that they would have a better time with *Taxi Driver*.

In mid-1973, when ex-agent David Begelman became President of Columbia Pictures, he wanted Hollywood to notice. Begelman was a paradox: a well-liked man who understood the "talent," and yet (it later transpired), a petty crook as well. The studio boss who turned up his nose at the sordid side of *Taxi Driver* was an embezzler who—despite earning a huge salary—had been creaming money off his bosses. He was a gambler and forger who ended up facing grand theft felony charges. It was both ironic and strangely apt that he was the executive who (however reluctantly) eventually greenlit *Taxi Driver*.

Begelman, who committed suicide in a Los Angeles hotel in August 1995, embodied many of the contradictions of 1970s America. This was the Watergate era, a time when even the most respected figures in the most prestigious jobs turned out to have dirty hands. *Taxi Driver* reflected the unease the American people felt about their politicians. In Charles Panatine (Leonard Harris in a role originally intended for Rock Hudson), the unctuous would-be president that Travis Bickle dreams of assassinating, *Taxi Driver* has its own sullied version of a Nixon—or a Begelman.

In 1973, Begelman's record was clean. He wanted to establish his credentials as studio tycoon. Striking a two-movie deal with coveted husband and wife team Julia and Michael Phillips seemed a smart way to do it. True, he detested *Taxi Driver*, the first of the two films, but the second project had promise. Also written by Paul Schrader, it was called *Watch the Skies*. In Begelman's opinion, this was the banker. Steven Spielberg, an old client from Begelman's days as an agent, was assigned to direct. Spielberg quickly rewrote

Schrader's screenplay and retitled it *Close Encounters of the Third Kind*. He was thinking big. Columbia's shareholders were startled at the size of budget he was seeking for his sci-fi epic, but Begelman was convinced "CE3K" (as it became known in studio memos) was a box-office winner. Almost as an afterthought, he allowed the Phillipses to move ahead with *Taxi Driver*. Even if it failed, he seemed to be reasoning, it was not going to cost much. Besides, Scorsese, Schrader, and De Niro were practically giving away their services for free. It was later revealed that their combined upfront fees for the film amounted to less than $130,000. (At the time, all could have earned fortunes if they had broken the deal to make the movie and accepted other assignments instead.)

Even so, Columbia was taking a risk. "You couldn't make *Taxi Driver* today," Schrader commented in 2005. "And you couldn't make it at a studio for sure. But it was such a time of flux for the movies. They [the studios] were taking chances on filmmakers. Today, we remember the great films that came out of that, but a lot of bad films came out of it too. For every *Taxi Driver*, there is a *Strawberry Statement* [1970] or a *Last Movie* [1971]. But there was a brief window that was open."

In one sense, the film is a twisted homage to New York. Travis Bickle may have detested the place (the first time we hear his narration, he is thanking God for "the rain which has helped wash the garbage and trash off the sidewalks"), but for the filmmakers it was a source of inspiration, even at its most squalid and oppressive. "There is something about the summertime in New York that is extraordinary," Scorsese told critics David Thompson and Ian Christie. "We shot the film during a very hot summer and there's an atmosphere at night that's like a seeping kind of virus. You can smell it in the air and taste it in your mouth ... a strange disease creeps along the streets of the city and, while we were shooting the film, we would slide along after it. Many times people threatened us and we had to take off quickly."

The New York that Travis lives in (and that Scorsese and his crew were shooting in) was a metropolis coming apart at the seams. In late June 1975, just around the time production was beginning, the city was on the verge of bankruptcy. Orders were issued to dismiss 19,000 city workers because there was no money to pay their salaries. In his book, *Maximum City*, Michael Pye offers an image of near-universal decay, violence, and corruption in mid-1970s New York: "There were fewer police; so there was nobody to bust the neighborhood drug supermarkets, or the numbers games that posted yesterday's winners in a storefront window and offered doughnuts and coffee while you waited. Firefighters on Staten Island changed shift in gypsy cabs. Parks became wilderness. Subways broke down ..."

It was not as if there was some idyllic moment in the city's recent past when things were better. New York's history, as Scorsese knew as well as anyone, was colorful, chaotic, and violent. *The Gangs of New York* (1927), Herbert Asbury's "informal history of the underworld" (which Scorsese was later to make into a film), portrayed the city of the 19th century in a carnivalesque but grim light, as a place where murder was commonplace, gangs fought bitter turf wars, and prostitution and drunkenness were rife. The rough, vibrant character of the city was a source of pride to local inhabitants.

In the prohibition era (the late 1920s), bootleggers and gangsters ran amok. When Scorsese was growing up, gang warfare remained widespread. In both *Who's That Knocking at My Door* (1968) and (more graphically) in *Mean Streets* (1973), the young filmmaker sought to capture the buzz and mayhem of everyday life on the streets of the Lower East Side.

For generations, the Mob had been entrenched in the life of the city and its environs. Scorsese's superb 1990 feature *Goodfellas* shows just how commonplace organized crime had become. Rather than focus on epic gun battles and *Scarface*-like feats of flamboyance, the film concentrated on the inner workings of the Mob: the clothes the wise guys wore, the food they ate, their argot, and their camaraderie. "As far back as I can remember," the opening voice-over begins, "I'd always wanted to be a gangster ... to be a somebody in a neighborhood full of nobodies." Scorsese describes the film as being "like a staged documentary." It introduces a range of characters who might have escaped from the pages of Damon Runyon, the supreme chronicler of New York lowlife. Characters like Frankie the Wop, Pete the Killer, and Jimmy Two-Times are paraded in front of the cameras. Although Scorsese relishes the chance to satirize them, to mock their bad skin, oafish manners, and social pretensions, it is evident that these men are part of the fabric of New York life.

New York is not just famous for gangsters, violence, and corruption. Paradoxically, it is also known and celebrated as the most tolerant city in the US. Writer, actor, and comedian Spalding Gray perhaps summed it up best when he explained his reasons for living there. "I knew I couldn't live in America and I wasn't ready to move to Europe so I moved to an island off the coast of America—New York City ... it was tolerant. It was a place that tolerated differences and could incorporate them and embrace them, which was what America was supposed to be about and wasn't."

Gray called New York "an insane angel ... completely, hugely in your face" and "a human miracle." He pointed out the fact that New York "continues in the face of all of the chaos, of the crime, of the madness, you just think that it would just pop and vanish, just explode."

New York was a city in which just about everyone could be assimilated—except Travis Bickle. In the years since *Taxi Driver* was made, it has become increasingly apparent that there is a rift in US society between the puritanical heartland and the permissive, media-savvy big cities. During the 1990s, there was a marked growth in nationalism and Christian fundamentalism. More and more Travis Bickle types were perpetrating horrific acts to defend a conservative set of values they felt was under threat in the new America. In the spring of 1995, a 27-year-old right-wing zealot, ex-soldier, and gun enthusiast called Timothy McVeigh helped bomb the Alfred P. Murrah Federal Building in Oklahoma City, killing 168 people. His motive, he told *Time* magazine, was that he was "angered" at the way the US government had behaved during the siege at Waco.

Between 1996 and 1998, Eric Rudolph, another ex-soldier with right-wing leanings, fundamentalist Christian beliefs, and a hatred of homosexuality, prostitution, and abortion, had bombed (or attempted to bomb) gay nightclubs, abortion clinics, and even the Atlanta Olympic Games.

Rudolph and McVeigh were far from unique. There were many others who shared their ideology and imitated their crimes. The closeness of the 2000 and 2004 US presidential elections suggested a country that was split down the middle. Issues such as abortion, euthanasia, homosexual marriage, and terrorism polarized the country.

Taxi Driver anticipates (and dramatizes) the divisions that were shortly to open up within US society. Travis, the fictional out of towner dreamed up by the Calvinist-raised Schrader, shares many of the values of the real-life bombers, assassins, and ideologues who would follow him. His disdain toward New York has long been shared in the United States' bible-belt. With its huge ethnic population and tradition of tolerance and assimilation, the city is—as Spalding Gray would have it—an anomaly. When Travis embarks on his mission to clean the filth off the sidewalk, he is doing just what evangelical leaders in the Midwest have long been advocating. In his own warped way, he stands for a set of puritan values that are as old as the US itself. What makes *Taxi Driver* so intriguing is that we are never quite sure how closely the filmmakers identify with those values.

The New York of *Taxi Driver* is very different from the world shown in Scorsese's gangster films. Maybe it is the heat, but nerves are frayed and tension is rising. In this city, cuckolded husbands threaten to turn into killers. Scorsese's own, deeply unsettling cameo captures the oppressive mood of the film. The director's decision to appear in his own movie was driven by necessity, not the desire to leave a Hitchcock-style signature behind him. When George Memmoli, the actor originally cast, failed to show up, the director took the role instead.

Night-time New York evoked in the Taxi Driver poster, in a style reminiscent of the paintings of Edward Hopper.

Martin Scorsese on location in 1973 for his previous New York masterpiece Mean Streets.

Robert De Niro in his seminal role as the trigger-happy John "Johnny Boy" Civello in Mean Streets.

Leading man Robert De Niro and director Martin Scorsese on the set of Taxi Driver.

The film describes the increasing isolation of loner Travis Bickle as he spends his off-duty hours in porn cinemas.

At the wheel of his cab Travis is insulated—and alienated—from the life he sees on the streets of New York City. As disdain turns to disgust, he sees the "scum" around him as something to be dealt with; if society can't, he will.

Cybill Shepherd as the vapid presidential campaign worker Betsy, here with Tom played by Albert Brooks.

Harvey Keitel as the pimp "Sport" Matthew with his teenage prostitute Iris played by Jodie Foster.

Martin Scorsese (right) directs Robert De Niro and Cybill Shepherd on the set of the election campaign office.

What became an iconic shot of Jodie Foster, in her controversial role as the underage hooker Iris Steensma.

Travis connects with Iris and her unnamed friend (played by Garth Avery), seeing their situation as a symptom of the sickness in society that he then sets out to address.

Keitel and De Niro: "Sport" Matthew confronts taxi driver Travis, who's on a mission to save the young Iris.

One of the most enduring shot of De Niro's seminal anti-hero as he rehearses his assassination attempt.

A shaven-headed Travis Bickle on the homicidal rampage which constitutes the violent conclusion to the movie.

The bristling intensity with which Scorsese plays the jilted husband, raging in the back of Travis's cab, gives us a sense of his state of mind during the shooting of *Taxi Driver*. He makes Travis pull the cab over to the curb. As they stay parked with the meter still running, the two men stare at an apartment window. "Cabbie, ya see that light up there on the seventh floor ... ya see that woman there? That's my wife ... but it ain't my apartment ... a nigger lives there," Scorsese snarls out before telling Travis that he is going to kill her with a .44 magnum. "Did you ever see what it can do to a woman's pussy, cabbie? I'm going to put it right up to her, cabbie. Right in her, cabbie. You must think I'm real sick, huh? A real pervert. Sitting here talking about a woman's pussy and a .44."

It is a repulsive scene, but one rich in irony. For just a moment, Travis seems sensible and level-headed, at least by comparison with his foul-mouthed passenger. However, the passenger's words strike a chord with him. The potent mix of racism, prurience, and machismo in the passenger's mini-rant appeals to Travis's own prejudices.

Disconcertingly, by the time Senator Palantine is in the back of the cab and canvassing Travis's opinion about how to improve the country, Travis is beginning to sound like a biblical avenger. In the Bible's Book of Jude, we hear of Sodom and Gomorrah "and the cities about them in like manner, giving themselves over to fornication and going after strange flesh," thereby risking the vengeance of "eternal fire." In the book of Travis Bickle, we hear appeals to clean up the city. "It's full of filth and scum, scum and filth. It's like an open sewer. Sometimes I can hardly take it ... we need a president who would clean up this whole mess."

Immediately after his encounter with the senator, Travis takes Betsy, a campaign worker for Palantine, on a disastrous date to a porno movie in Times Square. If there is any inconsistency in railing against sleaze one moment and going to watch sex films the next, Travis does not seem to appreciate it. His film of choice is called *Sometime Sweet Susan* (1974), playing in a double bill with *Swedish Marriage Manual*. The film guides do not have much to relate about the movie. "Young woman with double personality is sent to an asylum, where she starts having sexual fantasies with her psychiatrist and, sometimes, her nurse," reads the potted synopsis as given on the website "The Internet Movie Database."

Scorsese and Schrader do not explain why Travis takes Betsy to such a sordid dive. The scene is both comic and squalid. There is a sense that Travis relishes rubbing Betsy's nose in the dirt of Times Square. She is a clean-living, middle-class woman and he wants to drag her down, even at the risk of sabotaging their relationship. Then again, he claims (perhaps truthfully) that "all kinds of couples" go to such movies. When *Taxi Driver* was made, the notorious porno movie *Deep Throat* (1972), starring Linda Lovelace, was still on widespread release. It was the first sex film to achieve wide, mainstream acceptance. Middle-class couples talked about it at dinner parties. Celebrities endorsed the film. The fact that it was a hardcore, low-budget exploitation pic (much like *Sometime Sweet Susan*) was overlooked. Nor did the audiences clamoring to see it worry that the film was funded with gangland money.

Even if parts of middle-class America were fascinated by the murky underworld represented by Lovelace, there was a widespread sense of fear and revulsion about the way that the red-light districts were eating into the core of major cities. Thirty years on, the authorities have made a concerted attempted to reclaim their lawless streets. With his zero tolerance/broken windows policies, controversial New York mayor Rudy Giuliani did exactly what Travis Bickle begged Senator Palantine to do: "to clean up this city here. It's full of filth and scum; scum and filth. It's like an open sewer ... flush it out."

Whether Giuliani's motives were as altruistic as he claimed and what the social consequences of his policies were for New York's most vulnerable citizens are still a matter of heated debate. Nonetheless, the neon-lit, sleaze-filled city of Travis Bickle's day has been changed almost beyond recognition. Times Square is now full of offices, shops, and legitimate businesses.

"*Taxi Driver*, a quintessential New York movie ... today looks as if it might have been lensed on Mars," the *Village Voice* reported in an article entitled "The Vanishing New York Of *Taxi Driver*." Most of the landmarks in Travis Bickle's New York, whether the strip joints or the cafes, are long since destroyed or replaced by more respectable businesses.

Schrader acknowledges that the city has probably changed for the better. "My office is right in the heart of the new Times Square, the theme-park Times Square, but the old Times Square was pretty fucking scary. You wouldn't go down 42nd Street. It was all drug dealers and hookers—and I don't know how nostalgic you can be for that."

Still, it has not been possible to erase entirely the city through which Travis roamed. The presence in Times

Square in 2005 of a US Army recruitment station may be incongruous, but it hints at anxieties that are even more pronounced today than they were 30 years ago. In the wake of 9/11 and the destruction of the World Trade Center, the fear of the "other" that paralyzed Travis is shared by huge swathes of the US population. The porno theaters may be gone, but the threat of violence is still there. The mini-apocalypse wrought by that New York City fundamentalist Travis Bickle seems utterly inconsequential by comparison with the real-life tragedy that cost close to 3,000 lives in a single morning.

Walk a few blocks down from Times Square toward the Port Authority bus station and the Garment District and you quickly realize that much of the dirt and squalor of 1970s New York is still there: it has just been brushed a little farther out of sight of the tourists. On street corners, you will see crippled army veterans begging for small change. It is also not so hard to find stores selling hardcore sex videos and DVDs. Tramps, tarot card readers, and street vendors selling cheap and wretched merchandise are forever hustling tourists. The buildings are gray and shabby, with broken windows and derelict fire escapes. They are also so high and so narrow that the sunshine struggles to penetrate.

Schrader has talked about the near telepathic relationship he, Scorsese, and De Niro enjoyed during the making of the film. "There wasn't a whole lot of talk about what does this mean? Does it make sense? We knew it. It was a part of our private logic. Why does Travis Bickle take Betsy to a porn movie? What do you mean why? He does, he does. That is the answer."

For all the struggles to get the film financed and completed, and the fight to secure an R certificate, Scorsese had been in a privileged position. He was largely left to his own devices. As Julia Phillips noted, there were no previews or test screenings with carefully selected groups of teenagers. "The guys with no opinions—marketing mavens—haven't completely taken over yet, so we just keep showing it [the film] to our friends. We know the movie is working when there is gasping, no laughing."

critical reaction

We are so accustomed to the idea of *Taxi Driver* as one of the classics of 1970s cinema that it comes as a surprise to learn how hostile some critics were toward the film on its initial release. True, Scorsese had some powerful champions. Pauline Kael, *The New Yorker*'s critic and arguably the most influential writer on film in the US at the time, warmed to what she called "the seamy, rich pulpiness" of the movie. "No other film has ever dramatized urban indifference so powerfully; at first, here, it's horrifyingly funny, and then just horrifying," she wrote, praising Scorsese's immaculate handling of his cast.

Nor was Kael discomfited by the violence. "This film doesn't operate on the level of moral judgment of what Travis does. Rather, by drawing us into his vortex it makes us understand the psychic discharge of the quiet boys who go berserk," she suggested. Intriguingly, her reading of the film's coda, in which Travis is pacified and back behind the wheel of his cab, was not that Travis was cured, "but that the city is crazier than he is."

The New York *Times*' Vincent Canby had the ability to sink a movie at birth. His notorious review of the three-and-a-half-hour cut of Michael Cimino's *Heaven's Gate* (1980) was a case in point. "*Heaven's Gate* fails so completely that you might suspect Mr Cimino sold his soul to the Devil to obtain the success of *The Deer Hunter* [1978] and the Devil has just come around to collect,"

Canby wrote. He also likened the film to taking "a forced, four-hour walking tour of one's own living room." Within days of his review appearing, United Artists withdrew the film from circulation before re-releasing it in a much shortened version.

Canby was one of the most caustic and hard-to-please film critics around, but De Niro's "riveting" performance won him over to *Taxi Driver*. He called it "a vivid, galvanizing portrait of a character so particular that you may be astonished he makes consistent dramatic sense ... he is more than a character who is certifiably insane. He is a projection of all our nightmares of urban alienation, refined in a performance that is effective as much for what Mr De Niro does as for how he does it. Acting of this sort is rare in films. It is a display of talent, which one gets in the theater, as well as a demonstration of behavior, which is what movies usually offer."

Time magazine's Richard Schickel offered a far harsher assessment. For him, Travis was "more a case study" than a full-blown character. Scorsese, he argued, had offered the movie equivalent of a Sunday supplement piece on the mind of the assassin. "Unfortunately," Schickel concluded, "social comment does not come easily to him, and the strain shows. It is a conflict he can resolve only in a violence that seems forced and—coming after so much dreariness—ridiculously pyrotechnical."

In Europe, the response was equally mixed. British critics were fascinated and appalled in equal measure by Scorsese's bloody morality tale when it opened in late August 1976, in the same week as Alfred Hitchcock's final feature, *Family Plot*.

Hitchcock was one of Scorsese's idols, but the well-mannered murder mystery *Family Plot* saw him working at something less than full throttle. There was a sense of transition, even of an oedipal struggle. Scorsese, representing the new guard, was toppling the old Hollywood that Hitchcock represented. As the *Sunday Telegraph* noted, *Taxi Driver* was a young man's film, "full of moral indignation that batters at the senses and almost implodes the story's momentum," while Hitchcock's swansong was "cool, immoral, and humorous."

One of the more perceptive reviews, by Derek Malcolm in the *Guardian*, pointed out that the film's very obvious flaws were what made it so rich and fascinating. Malcolm denied that *Taxi Driver* was any kind of "imperishable masterpiece to be approached on bended knee by critics," but stated that its power and importance lay in "the urgency with which it is made."

The *Observer*'s Russell Davies was struck by the obvious contradiction at the heart of the film: that it leaves the audience with a public hero in whom "a crackling monster still dwells. We know he is to be feared. But there is nothing we can do with that knowledge. That's what's so sinister and frustrating about the film. It transfers Travis's burden of impotent fear and disgust to us."

"Hellishly brilliant," opined the *Evening News* of *Taxi Driver*. "Fighting back nausea, I was stunned with admiration at the incredible virtuosity and high surface gloss Scorsese gets on his work." "A Taxi Ride To Terror," was the headline of the review in mass-market paper the *Sun*. "Go on, take this nasty ride," advised the *Sunday People*. However, the *Daily Mail* grumbled about "the taxi that didn't take me anywhere" while the *Financial Times* called *Taxi Driver* "luridly overwritten" and "Scorsese's worst film to date." The *FT* went on to bemoan "the laboriousness" with which the film served up its sermon on "the seeds of fascism" and called the subplot about political assassination "a ludicrous dead-end."

Such squibs would hardly have surprised the filmmaker. Given the subject matter, it was well-nigh inevitable that certain reviewers would take against *Taxi Driver*. For Scorsese and Schrader, more hurtful was a long piece, "The Power and the Gory," cowritten by Manny Farber and his wife Patricia Patterson in the pages of the US movie magazine *Film Comment*. Interviewed in early 2005, Schrader acknowledged that he still could not bring himself to read the article.

An artist and academic as well as a critic, Farber worked on a different level to the reviewers turning out quick pieces for the newspapers and magazines. He engaged with the movies he was writing about in a far more profound (and eccentric) way. He used to watch films again and again; project them backward or without sound, pore over them until he felt he understood their essence.

Farber and Patterson found much to admire in *Taxi Driver*: the Baroque, constantly bold visuals, Scorsese's "nervous-generous hoopla of techniques," and the "assaulting quality" with which Scorsese told Travis Bickle's story. (They likened his approach to "a gnat banging suicidally against the light fixture.")

Always keen on music metaphors, especially those drawn from jazz, Farber and Patterson talked of the "jamming of styles: Fritz Lang expression, Bresson's distanced realism, and

Corman's low-budget horrifics." Nonetheless, they could not help pointing out some of the non-sequiturs in the movie: the way that Travis's cab never ran out of petrol or got caught in traffic jams, the fact that he could gun down a black thief in a convenience store without the cops noticing, the strange transformation of the psychopathic killer into "a liberating hero by the New York press."

Travis, they noted, was a deeply inconsistent character: "a whirligig with his IQ and sophistication shifting and sliding all over the place." More worryingly, they spotted something noxious at the core of the film. "Every frame is awash with prejudices of take-the-law-into-your-hands fare: the idea of sex as transaction, in which all the barely differentiated women are professional manipulators of men; black people are animalistic sinisters who get the sexual goodies and call the sexual shots; the lower class patronized as animals feeding on each other." Nor did they care for the way *Taxi Driver* fetishized and worshipped the gun or the way it "played both sides of the box-office dollar: obeisance to the box-office provens, such as concluding on a ten-minute massacre ..." while at the same time making its nods to European auteur cinema and the work of experimental filmmakers like Michael Snow.

Early on in *Taxi Driver*, Travis Bickle stops to have a coffee with his colleagues in a greasy spoon cafe. "The thick smell hangs in the air—fried grease, smoke, sweat, regurgitated wine ... whatever doesn't flush away in New York at night turns up in places like this," Schrader's screenplay instructs us. It is late at night and the cab drivers are shooting the breeze, talking about sex and money. Travis takes the corner seat, as far away as he can get from Charlie T., the one black cab driver. Travis eyes him suspiciously and merely nods blankly when Wizard (Peter Boyle) tries to effect an introduction. He tells Wizard about an assault that has just taken place on a driver on 122nd Street, the heart of black New York. "Fucking Mau Mau land," Wizard sneers.

We see Travis gazing around the cafe. The camera pans across the cafe in slow motion. Among the customers, looking very intimidating indeed, are two immaculately dressed black men, both presumably pimps. One is in a white shirt and white hat. The other is in a dark suit and dark hat. He is lazily tapping the table as a waitress places a beer in front of him. Travis looks at him with a mix of suspicion and loathing. One of his colleagues asks him if he carries "a piece ... it's a good thing to have just as a threat." It is at this point that something seems to go click in Travis's mind. We see him drop some Alka-Seltzers into a glass of water. Scorsese throws in an extreme close-up of the pills fizzing and dissolving, turning the water white. Travis, we infer, is beginning to think some very murderous thoughts. His fear of the "other" is unsettling him.

In Schrader's original screenplay, Travis's racism was even more explicitly foregrounded. Sport (Harvey Keitel), the bandana-wearing pimp who becomes the focus for Travis's murderous revenge fantasies, was originally intended to be a black character. "We felt there might be riots and violence in theaters if we went that way," Schrader later remarked of the decision to make the character white. He and Scorsese do not attempt to conceal the fact that Travis is a racist character. Nonetheless, they did agree to take "the really incendiary stuff" out of the movie.

On one level, *Taxi Driver* can be seen as a fascist parable. Travis, the vulnerable, frightened little white man, not long back from the war and eking out an existence in a city in flux, is not so far removed from the impoverished young Corporal Hitler adrift in Munich at the end of World War I. Just as Hitler began to steep himself in antisemitic literature and propaganda, Travis comes up with his own rhetoric about cleaning "the scum" off the sidewalk.

For many critics, the most unsettling aspect of *Taxi Driver* is its ambivalent attitude toward its own racist antihero. However obliquely, Scorsese and Schrader risk endorsing Travis's skewed political vision. "Racism is the problem with which *Taxi Driver* never quite comes to terms. And this evasion prevents it from being a truly great film," critic Amy Taubin wrote in an influential essay on the film (published as part of the British Film Institute's "Film Classics" series). The filmmakers countered her charge, pointing out that there is an obvious difference between making a film about a racist and making a racist movie.

Nonetheless, it is striking that *Taxi Driver* has no sympathetic or even remotely complex black characters. There is something perverse and perhaps implausible about Travis Bickle's choice of profession. For somebody obsessed with race and distrustful of blacks, cab driving is a crazy career option. As the statistics in the *New York Taxicab Fact Book* make clear, this is "an immigrant industry." In the period 1990 to 2003, 89 percent of new drivers were immigrants, born in 84 foreign countries. Many were of African or Caribbean origin. During this period, 60 languages were spoken among driver applicants. Although most immigrant applicants learned English once they had come to the US, "less than half (43%) said they spoke English at home (even in addition to their native language). *Taxi Driver* doesn't even begin to reflect this reality. In the Belmore cafeteria or at the depot, every driver is a fluent English speaker. Scorsese and Schrader have airbrushed the immigrants out of the picture in the same way that they have ignored or demonized the black characters. *Taxi Driver* may occasionally seem like a piece of blue-collar realism, but the filmmakers have made little attempt to do justice to the ethnic diversity of New York's *Taxi Driver* population," wrote Amy Taubin.

As stated earlier, one of the richest aspects of the movie is its many detailed, finely nuanced performances. From Albert Brooks as the smug, yuppie political campaign worker and Keitel as the pimp, to Jodie Foster as the 12-year-old prostitute and Peter Boyle as the philosophical cab driver, *Taxi Driver* abounds in raw, lively protagonists who are credible precisely because they are so contradictory. Contrast this with the cursory and suspicious way in which Scorsese and Schrader treat black characters. They are either shown in passing (like the overdressed pimps in the all-night cafe), gunned down (Travis turning vigilante, have-a-go-hero in a grocery store), or referred to in stereotypical ways (witness Scorsese's cameo as the cuckolded husband, sitting outside the apartment where his wife is cheating on him—"a nigger lives there," he snarls at Travis).

The irony is that *Taxi Driver* shares several of the hallmarks of the blaxploitation cycle of the early 1970s. Films like *Superfly* (1972), *Coffy* (1973), and *Foxy Brown* (1974) were also violent, urban tales, full of pimps, prostitutes, and alienated outsiders.

A decade after *Taxi Driver*, Spike Lee tried to hire Robert De Niro to play the Italian-American pizza owner in his 1988 feature *Do the Right Thing*. (The role was eventually taken by Danny Aiello.) This was a movie that owed a clear debt to *Taxi Driver*. It, too, was set in New York during a sweltering summer and showed how the tensions simmering beneath the surface of the city could soon boil up into violence. Just as Scorsese and Schrader had been accused of ignoring the experiences of black New Yorkers, Lee was attacked for tilting the balance unfairly against the white characters. The movie ends with a race riot in which the pizza restaurant is razed. Lee shows little sympathy for the owner. Whether or not *Do the Right Thing* was balanced, at least it gave a voice to New York's black-American community—something *Taxi Driver* conspicuously failed to do.

Scorsese's detractors did not just pick up on the ambivalent treatment of the black characters in *Taxi Driver*. They also pointed out that the film was about as muddled up and paradoxical as its lead character. The irony was that many of *Taxi Driver's* champions would go along with such an assessment. *Taxi Driver* was nothing if not contradictory. In interviews given then and afterward, Scorsese and Schrader were at pains to say that the film reflected their state of mind at the time it was conceived.

It is important to put *Taxi Driver* in context. This was one of a number of movies made in the mid-1970s that seemed to be driven by a cold, righteous fury against the establishment. These films did not necessarily offer a coherent critique of the social or political problems of the era, but they did make it patently clear how widespread the disaffection with authority (whether represented by police or politicians) had become. "If some people approve of what he [Travis] did, they're nuts. There are nuts up there on the screen. I can't help it if there are nuts in the audience too," Scorsese told the *Guardian* in a 1976 interview. "Those who call it a fascist film have to be joking. It's about a man who takes the fascist way out, if you like. And it doesn't exactly blame him because how can you blame a man like that?"

Scorsese had always wanted *Taxi Driver* to create controversy. In interviews, he himself courted it, speaking language so extreme one guessed that Schrader was lurking out of sight, scripting it for him. Not that the anger they were venting was unusual. In the mid-1970s, there were plenty of other soapbox orators and would-be Savonarolas, keen to expose the iniquities of the society around them. Nor was Travis unique in Hollywood movies of the time. Peter Finch's newscaster turned demagogue in Sidney Lumet's *Network* (1976), shot in New York at almost the same time as *Taxi Driver*, was a soulmate of sorts for Travis Bickle.

Stylistically poles apart, *Taxi Driver* and *Network* are nonetheless both tapping into the same fury and disaffection that existed in the US of the mid-1970s. "I'm mad as hell and I'm not going to take it any more," Howard Beale (Finch) roars at the watching millions when he goes off the rails during a newscast. He even sets a date for his own suicide on air. His speech is worth quoting in detail because it articulates feelings that Travis shared, too.

"I don't have to tell you things are bad," Beale roars at his startled viewers. "Everybody knows things are bad. It's a depression. Everybody's out of work or scared of losing their job. The dollar buys a nickel's work, banks are going bust, shopkeepers keep a gun under the counter. Punks are running wild in the street and there's nobody anywhere who seems to know what to do, and there's no end to it. We know the air is unfit to breathe and our food is unfit to eat, and we sit watching our TV's while some local newscaster tells us that today we had 15 homicides and 63 violent crimes, as if that's the way it's supposed to be. We know things are bad—worse than bad. They're crazy. It's like everything everywhere is going crazy, so we don't go out anymore. We sit in the house, and slowly the world we are living in is getting smaller, and all we say is, 'Please, at least leave us alone in our living rooms' ... Well, I'm not gonna leave you alone. I want you to get mad! ... You've got to say, 'I'm a human being. Goddamnit! My life has value!' So I want you to get up now. I want all of you to get up out of your chairs. I want you to get up right now and go to the window. Open it, and stick your head out, and yell, 'I'm as mad as hell, and I'm not going to take this anymore!'"

Network had been written by Paddy Chayevsky, one of the writers who revolutionized TV drama in the US in the 1950s. Chayevsky's most important work was *Marty*, broadcast live on NBC's *Television Playhouse* in May 1953, and subsequently made into a film. Chayevsky's achievement was to create a central character who was neither good-looking nor successful and did not have success with women. At a time when advertisers and sponsors were lobbying for glossy, escapist drama to put viewers in the mood to buy the goods they hawked between the programs, this was a radical gesture. On TV, Marty, the lovelorn butcher with the domineering mother, was played by Rod Steiger, an actor with a brooding intensity matching that of De Niro.

Of course, it would be fanciful to suggest a direct link between the ungainly New York butcher and Travis Bickle two decades later, but Chayevsky and fellow writers like Rod Serling (*Requiem for a Heavyweight*, 1962) and Reginald Rose (*12 Angry Men*, 1957) pioneered a new realism. They made it possible for filmmakers to tell grueling, downbeat stories about small-timers. Marty may not have been quite as disaffected as Travis Bickle, but he was a character in a similar mold.

Sidney Lumet, who directed *Network* and who had cut his teeth as a filmmaker during the so-called "Golden Age" of TV drama in the 1950s, had long been prepared to make films about alienated outsiders, chafing against a society that marginalized them. Lumet's *Dog Day Afternoon* (1975) shared some of the same hallmarks as *Taxi Driver*. It was based on a true story. On the afternoon of August 22nd, 1972, John Woltowicz attempted to rob a branch of the Chase Manhattan Bank in Brooklyn. He wanted money to pay for his lover's sex change operation. The heist went disastrously wrong and Woltowicz ended up holding hostages in the bank, besieged by the New York police force outside. As played by Al Pacino, Woltowicz was another character with the same mix of bravado and naivete as Travis Bickle.

Also released in 1975 was Milos Forman's *One Flew Over the Cuckoo's Nest*. In R.P. McMurphy (Jack Nicholson), the rebel locked up in a mental asylum, it boasted a hero as iconic for his times as Travis Bickle. Whereas Travis was introspective, lonely, and alienated, McMurphy was cheerful and gregarious. "As near as I can figure out, it's because I fight and fuck too much," he tells the doctor who asks just what he is doing in a mental institution. He is 38 years old, with five counts of assault and one of statutory rape against him. "Between you and me, she might have been 15, but when you get that little red beaver right out there in front of you I don't think it's crazy at all ... no man alive could resist that. That's why I got into jail to begin with and now they're telling me I'm crazy because I don't sit there like a goddamned vegetable." The prison authorities believe he has been faking insanity to get off his work detail and have sent him to the asylum for observation. That is the starting point.

McMurphy expresses his indignation against the system in a very different way than Travis. Rather than resort to violence, he takes his fellow inmates on an illicit fishing trip. Nevertheless, McMurphy is another example of the outsider as hero or antihero. In 1970s US cinema, the Travis Bickles, Howard Beales, and R.P. McMurphys were foregrounded at the expense of the old-style clean-cut, clean-living leading men. The difference about Travis Bickle was that he was revealed in the least flattering light. As Schrader stated at an early press conference for *Taxi Driver*: "We show you the underside of the characters that were viewed superficially in *Dog Day Afternoon* and *One Flew Over the Cuckoo's Nest*. These were not easy movies to finance, but still Pacino and Nicholson only gave you the cutesy, ingratiating side of the characters they played. De Niro gets what they were afraid to. You see that Travis is not to be tolerated. He should be killed."

In an interview with *Time Out* in the late 1990s, Scorsese recalled that the first time he met Schrader, the screenwriter had a gun on the table. "He had alienated everybody, like a kamikaze, do or die. And that's what that script is. It's full of rage and anger. I was too. I can't speak for De Niro, but he saw something in it. I believed in making that film to the death. It was the worst shooting experience of my life making that film, to do honor to the script, because of the energy that went into it and what it represented. I kind of identified with it ... When I was younger, particularly, the anger and rage were so strong, it funneled itself right into that story. Ultimately, the difference is that Travis acts out his fantasy. He's on a spiritual road, but it's the wrong road. It's the road of annihilation and destruction, and there's no coming back."

Echoing Scorsese, Schrader acknowledged in an interview with *Film Comment* that *Taxi Driver* was a movie full of sound and fury, but one made with an adolescent sensibility. "*Taxi Driver* was written when I couldn't really distinguish between the pain in the work and the pain in my life ... *Taxi Driver* is a very rich piece of juvenilia, but it is juvenilia, it is an adolescent, immature mind struggling to identify itself. It has no maturity except at the talent level. It's like the ending of any rough, first adolescent work."

Maybe the film was critic-proof precisely because of this adolescent sensibility. Kids had turned out to see *Taxi Driver* in vast numbers. "The sheer violence of it really brought out the Times Square crowd," Schrader later noted. These moviegoers could not have cared less about what Vincent Canby or Pauline Kael had to say on the subject of the movie.

Often, films that are acclaimed as masterpieces on their initial release are quickly forgotten. Scan the list of Best Picture Oscar winners over the years and it is surprising how many lumpen or plain dreary efforts have been feted. By the same token, films that provoke, irritate, and get under the skin at an initial viewing often seem to improve with age. *Taxi Driver* falls into the latter category.

In Britain, in the mid-1980s, *Taxi Driver* was rereleased on a double bill with Alan Parker's *Midnight Express*. Parker's movie, scripted by Oliver Stone, was about Billy Hayes (Brad Davis), a young American languishing in an Istanbul jail after being busted trying to smuggle hash out of the country. In a key scene in the film, he gives a beating to the grizzled, slovenly Turkish prison warder. At the end of the sequence, Hayes has the warder pinioned on a staircase. In slow motion, we see the American crane his neck. He might almost be kissing his victim, but when he raises his head, we realize that he has just bitten out the benighted man's tongue. He spits it away. There is an extreme close-up of his face, streaked with blood and beaded with sweat. The look he is wearing is one of complete and utter exhilaration. That warder will never snitch on the prisoners again.

It is a testament to Parker's powers that we, too, share in Billy's frenzied joy. With its stylization, slow motion, and violence, *Midnight Express* must have seemed to distributors an apt partner for *Taxi Driver*. Nonetheless, watch the films side by side and it immediately becomes apparent that Scorsese's movie has a subtlety and richness that *Midnight*

Express cannot come close to matching. On repeated viewings, the flaws in *Midnight Express* (the bombast and the crude xenophobia) become ever more apparent. However, *Taxi Driver* simply seems to improve. The more you study it, the more you find in it.

"It is a film that does not grow dated or over-familiar. I have seen it dozens of times. Every time I see it, it works; I am drawn into Travis's underworld of alienation, loneliness, haplessness, and anger," Scorsese's long-time champion Roger Ebert wrote in a retrospective review in the *Chicago-Sun Times* in early 2004. In hindsight, he argued that the end sequence "plays like music, not drama: it completes the story on an emotional, not a literal level. We end not on carnage but on redemption, which is the goal of so many of Scorsese's characters. They despise themselves, they live in sin, they occupy "mean streets," but they want to be forgiven and admired. Whether Travis gains that status in reality or only in his mind is not the point, throughout the film his mental state has shaped his reality, and at last, in some way, it has brought him a kind of peace."

A surprisingly diverse group of filmmakers—some mainstream, some from the margins of art house cinema—have named *Taxi Driver* on their "Top 10 Movies of All Time" lists. Chen Kaige, the Chinese director of *Farewell My Concubine* (1993), championed the movie, as did Tarantino and (perhaps more susprisingly) the experimental Canadian director Atom Egoyan. Gary Fleder, director of big-budget Hollywood movies like *Kiss the Girls* (1997), *Don't Say a Word* (2001), and *Runaway Jury* (2003), gave an interview to the *Daily Telegraph* in 2004 bemoaning the fact filmmakers like himself simply were not given the chance to make movies as bold (and as ambiguous) as *Taxi Driver*. "If you wanted to pitch *Taxi Driver* to a studio today," Fleder said, "the first question they would ask is 'Where is the cop character? Where is the guy pursuing Travis? Where is the hero?' And if you said, 'He is the hero,' the studio would say, 'Well, go and shoot it on digital video, for no money, because no one will finance it.'"

taxi driver's legacy

In a short but revealing interview she gave to mark the 25th anniversary of *Taxi Driver*, Jodie Foster restated her loyalty to Scorsese and her pride in their work together. She argued passionately that *Taxi Driver* had "a moral center," and expressed her frustration that Hollywood had lost the knack for making such awkward and challenging films. "The best movies I know of were the 1970s precisely because people were really concerned or interested in the antihero," she said, "which has pretty much gone away now. I don't think audiences want to accept the antihero. So I do think that it [*Taxi Driver*] would be a movie which would be very difficult to finance today."

The actress's remarks were revealing. The very fact that she felt pressed to defend a movie that many saw as a masterpiece hinted at the firestorm *Taxi Driver* had caused. During the interview, Foster refused even to broach the subject with which Scorsese's film became indelibly (and unfairly) associated: John F. Hinckley Jr.'s 1981 assassination attempt on President Ronald Reagan.

There is a sense of Chinese boxes about a reclusive loner becoming inspired to carry out such a wanton and violent act as a result of a movie about a reclusive loner. Schrader's satirical digs at the cult of celebrity were clearly lost on the 26-year-old Oklahoma-born misfit, Hinckley. What drew him to *Taxi Driver* was the idea of killing a famous person and thereby validating himself in the eyes of a beautiful but unobtainable woman.

Born in May 1955, Hinckley was from a well-to-do family and had supportive parents. His father was a successful businessman in the oil and gas industry who moved the family to Dallas when John was four, before setting up home in Colorado. The Hinckleys were well connected. They knew the Bush family and were generous donators to George Bush Sr.'s first election campaign for US president. In John Hinckley's case, the usual arguments about the lone psychopath being part of a disenfranchized underclass simply did not apply, nor was there any evidence he was starved of affection or mistreated by his family.

Hinckley seemed like a reasonably well-adjusted kid until he reached adolescence. In high school, he became ever more reclusive. After he graduated, he enrolled in college, but soon dropped out and headed to Los Angeles. Living in a small apartment in Hollywood, he pursued his dream of becoming a musician. In 1976, he watched *Taxi Driver* 15 or more times. Later that year, wearying of what he called "the phony, impersonal Hollywood scene" (and presumably exasperated by his failure to make any kind of impact), he moved back to join his parents in Colorado, where they were then living. Just like would-be assassin Arthur Bremer, he took a menial job in a restaurant. Just like Travis Bickle, he became obsessed with guns. For the next three years, he drifted in and out of college, switching courses, never graduating, never making friends. His health suffered. He became depressed and started using tranquilizers.

To the distress of his parents, Hinckley flirted with right-wing politics, even briefly joining the American Nazi Party. He was thrown out for being too extreme. "He was a nut. He wanted to shoot people and blow things up," Michael Allen, president-elect of the extremist sect, told the press. At Texas Tech University, he was the first and only student to write a paper on Hitler's *Mein Kampf*. His professors were impressed by his thoroughness, but alarmed at his interest in the material. Showing a certain ideological inconsistency, he was also devoted to John Lennon and claimed to be devastated by Lennon's death, even if he did not pay too much attention to the former Beatle's creed about giving peace a chance.

It was at this point that his obsession with Jodie Foster was at its height. Learning that the actress was then studying at Yale, he started visiting the college campus, hanging around in the hope that he might bump into her. He bombarded the actress-turned-student with unsolicited love letters, some of which he pushed under her dorm door. He made five telephone calls to her that he recorded. "I'm not dangerous, I promise you that," he told her during one call, begging to be allowed to ring her again. "Oh God, oh seriously, this is really starting to bother me. Do you mind if I hang up?" Foster is heard to reply at the end of one of his calls.

Arthur Bremer's original quarry was President Nixon, but when he was thwarted, he switched his sights to Governor George Wallace instead. Hinckley's first target was President Carter. In the autumn of 1980, he began following Carter. In Nashville, where Carter was campaigning, he was arrested at the airport with various guns in his luggage. The authorities simply confiscated the guns and gave him a small fine. By now, Hinckley's parents knew that there was something deeply wrong with their son and sent him for sessions with a psychiatrist in Colorado. The shrink's verdict was that John was immature and needed to learn how to cope without parental handouts. He failed to realize that Hinckley needed more constraints, not fewer.

On March 30th, Hinckley made his assassination attempt on Reagan in Washington DC, emerging from a crowd of TV reporters to fire six shots at the president and his entourage. Reagan was hit in the chest. Several of his minders were also struck. Later, when the FBI raided Hinckley's hotel room, they discovered a virtual shrine to Foster. There was a letter from the would-be killer to Foster, written shortly before the shooting, in which he explained that his attempt to kill the president was motivated by the desire to impress her. His "historic act," as he called it, was supposed to show her that he loved her.

Back at Yale, Foster held a press conference, telling journalists that she had no regrets about any film she had ever done. The FBI, she revealed, had contacted her within minutes of the assassination attempt. "I felt very shocked, I felt very bad, frightened, distressed. I acted very badly, cried, I guess," she said of her first reaction to the news of Hinckley's actions.

After Hinckley's trial, at which he was found not guilty but insane, Foster's career briefly threatened to unravel. When she graduated from Yale in 1984, casting agents no longer seemed enthused about her. Foster put on weight and sank into a slough of depression. It was only in 1988, when she won her first Oscar for her performance in *The Accused*, that she reestablished herself. She played Sarah Tobias, a working-class waitress with a checkered past. According to the lawyers defending the men who gang-rape her, Sarah is of "questionable character." The fact that she had a messy private life, liked drink and drugs, and dressed flirtatiously meant—at least in the eyes of the legal system—that she "was asking for it."

The same double standard seemed to apply to Foster herself. In some subliminal way, she was partly blamed for Hinckley's actions—or, at least, tarred by her unwitting association with them. She was regarded not simply as an actress, but as a protagonist in an especially gruesome moment in recent US political history. She became the butt of crude jokes, was forced to retreat out of the public eye, and was then castigated for being aloof.

It was easy to understand why Foster grew so suspicious of the media. When US TV show 60 Minutes profiled Foster in April 2000 to tie in with the release of her film Anna and the King, she gave a wide-ranging interview in which she discussed her career in depth. By the time the show had been edited, audiences were led to believe that she had volunteered information about her feelings toward Hinckley. In fact, as she subsequently told journalist Rachel Abramowitz of US Weekly, the quotes had been taken out of context and given undue prominence. "They interviewed me for four and a half hours in my office. Maybe they asked me four questions about Hinckley. And of course the promo [for the show] comes out and it's all over the AP wires. 'Jodie reveals all about John Hinckley that she never has.'" In the same interview, Foster spoke of her dismay at the "gross" and "grotesque" fascination the public has with "celebrity pain." "Every time they do something like what *60 Minutes* did, it just turns me into a big misanthrope. 'Fine. I'm not going to talk to anybody about anything again. I can't trust anymore.'"

The Hinckley affair marked a grim postscript to *Taxi Driver*. Here was a film excoriating the violence within American society and satirizing the country's obsession with celebrity, and yet, five or six years after it was made, its critique seemed blunted. The film was already part of the culture it was attacking. "If some people approve of what he [Travis] did, they're nuts. There are nuts up there on the screen. I can't help it if there are nuts in the audience too," Scorsese complained in a 1976 interview with the *Guardian*. "Those who call it a fascist film have to be joking. It's about a man who takes the fascist way out, if you like. And it doesn't exactly blame him because how can you blame a man like that?"

It was not just Foster who became embroiled in Hinckley's murderous fantasies. As Paul Schrader revealed in an interview he gave at London's National Film Theatre in 1993, he also had a connection with the *Taxi Driver*-fixated psychopath. Schrader was in New Orleans shooting *Cat People* (1982) when Hinckley took his potshots at Reagan. He heard about the shooting on the car radio. By the time he got back to his hotel, FBI agents were waiting for him. They wanted to know if he had ever heard of Hinckley. Schrader replied in the negative.

"What they wanted to know is if I ever heard of him in connection with any other name. They were shooting off on conspiracies already," Schrader said. "The irony was that I did actually hear from him." Schrader had received one or two letters from a man in Colorado (Hinckley, it turned out) who wanted to meet Jodie Foster. His secretary told him about the letters. With his blessing, she threw them away.

When the FBI grilled him, Schrader realized that if he admitted having received the letters, he would become a part of the ongoing Hinckley soap opera. That was why he lied. "I didn't have the letters. I didn't even read the letters. My secretary was going to get involved and so I just said, no, I've never heard of him [Hinckley]."

As the *Taxi Driver* screenwriter acknowledged, Hinckley was far from unique. Just as Travis had inspired him, he spawned his own legion of copycats. Even if they did cite the movie as inspiration, Schrader disclaimed any responsibility for their actions. "I don't think I created that character [of Travis Bickle]," Schrader mused. "I think that character was afloat in the culture and certainly very much afloat in me. I think I seized him with such strength because of my personal identification with him. And I seized him with such strength that I captured him ... this is how art works. People see that thing [represented by Travis], recognize it, and then back away from it. That is how it worked in my own life. This repressed anger to strike out blindly was satiated by the fictional creation. For most viewers, they are satiated. For a man like John Hinckley who watched the movie over and over again, there is no line between him and the character he plays. That doesn't mean that it's the movie's fault. He could have gone to another movie just as well."

The idea that movies influence behavior is as old as cinema itself. Scorsese and Schrader would never deny that they were keen to get under the skin of their audiences, to provoke and discomfit them, but that was not the same as encouraging them to commit copycat, Travis Bickle-style killings. Even so, both men were caught in the middle of a ferocious debate about the media and violence in the wake of Hinckley's assassination attempt. They were accused of being part of a new generation of Hollywood "brutalists" who—as one academic put it—glorified and encouraged "the immense potential for savagery that already exists in America, attracting groups that will seek any match that will ignite their seething aggressions."

As Scorsese told J. Hoberman of *The Village Voice* in a rambling interview in the spring of 1976, blaming the filmmaker was like blaming the messenger. This was society's problem and showing violence was not the same as endorsing it. "*Taxi Driver* is about a man racked by dark feelings," he said. "I think everybody has them. It's unfortunate that some people act them out." What should we do, he asked in dismay, ban the film?

Perhaps the din surrounding *Taxi Driver* following the Hinckley incident would not have been quite so loud if the movie had ended in a different way. Scorsese and Schrader provided a highly ironic coda: in the final scene, Travis was back on the streets, driving his yellow cab. He may still have been "a nutcase" as Schrader called him, but the image of him seemingly contented, back behind the wheel, could not help but appear to legitimize his actions. Would Hinckley have copied Travis if he had shot himself (as he pretends to do with his bloodied finger after he committed his massacre of the pimps)?

Scorsese had been all too aware of the doubts about the ending of the movie even at the time of its release. As he told *The Village Voice*: "They [reviewers] don't understand the ending ... they're trying to find reasons why he did everything. And they get very upset at the ending because that may mean something else. See, everybody wants the picture to end like *Hamlet*, everybody's like dead all over the place, you know, and he [Travis] looks up and points a finger at his temple and shoots himself three times, you know. That's where everybody thinks it should end because it's just like a ... you know, I don't think a western is bad—I like westerns—somebody gets killed and everybody goes home. Everybody forgets about the picture."

Perhaps the reason that people do not forget *Taxi Driver* is that Travis did not die. The crumpled, bloodied figure in the mohawk survives. In a sense, this is a mark of yet another failure in Travis's life. Like Arthur Bremer, he clearly expected to be killed. Scorsese, always fond of his religious metaphors, talked about him making "a blood sacrifice of himself." In this case, the blood sacrifice is not accepted.

The 1976 *Village Voice* interview is especially revealing because it was given at a time when the film was still fresh in Scorsese's mind and before he had evolved the stock responses that he sometimes gave to questions about *Taxi Driver* in later years. The director admits that both he and Schrader identified very closely with Travis: "I think that he has right on the surface a lot of the emotions, a lot of the problems, that most everybody has in them. I have them,

Paul has 'em." In other words, Travis was not so much a psychopath as an everyman who had just been pushed a little bit too far. He embodied feelings that were commonplace in the society in which he lived—the rage behind the American Dream.

what happened next

After the stresses and trauma of their work together on *Taxi Driver*, it would have been understandable if Scorsese, De Niro, and Schrader had never worked together again. Instead, they plunged into a collaboration that turned out to be even more painful. Accounts of the making of *Raging Bull* (1980), a biopic about the middle-weight boxer Jake La Motta, make the fights between the filmmakers during *Taxi Driver* seem puny and half-hearted. Just as before, Schrader's script (written in conjunction with Mardik Martin) terrified studio execs with its violence and darkness. In his book *Final Cut*, Steven Bach, who had just taken over as head of United Artists, offers a comic account of his meeting with the filmmakers and their producer Irwin Winkler to figure out just how the script could be modified so that it would not be lumbered with a commercially suicidal X certificate. "What makes you so sure this is an X?" Bach is asked by the filmmakers. "When I read in a script 'CLOSE UP on Jake La Motta's erection as he pours ice water over it prior to the fight, then I think we're in the land of X," the studio chief replies.

Just as with Travis Bickle four or five years before, the studio chiefs fretted that no audience would want to see a movie about someone as downbeat, self-destructive, and generally unsympathetic as La Motta. Bach claimed that the script was extensively reworked in a way that made La Motta more of a human being and less of a "cockroach." He hints that De Niro (though uncredited) was behind the revised version of the screenplay that finally made United Artists prepared to greenlight *Raging Bull*. This seems plausible enough, if only because *Raging Bull* had been De Niro's pet project all along. He was the one who first gave Scorsese La Motta's autobiography and tried to talk him into making the movie.

Easy Riders, Raging Bulls, Peter Biskind's seminal study of the films (and excesses) of the era, offers a different thesis. According to Biskind, Schrader brought the human dimension to Jake La Motta who (in Mardik Martin's original draft) had been little more than a neanderthal. "We have to give Jake a depth, a stature he does not possess, otherwise he's not worth making a movie about," Schrader is reported to have told Scorsese. At first, the director demurred. Just as with Travis Bickle, he wanted to put a monster up on screen. That was part of the challenge he and De Niro set themselves: to portray a character who seems thoroughly repellent and yet to hint at his humanity. For Scorsese, the key was in the performance, not the dialog or storyline. It was up to his lead actor to win the audience over to La Motta.

Raging Bull is in a very different key to *Taxi Driver*. It is a full-blown American tragedy, a tale told on an epic scale. Nonetheless, it shares various hallmarks with its predecessor. There is the same strain of guilt and self-loathing. La Motta is not exactly an underground man in the way that Travis Bickle is, but he shares both Travis's self-destructive urges and his appetite for blood and violence. As with *Taxi Driver* and the "are you talkin' to me?" monolog, there is a pivotal scene that defines De Niro's performance and expresses in microcosm what the filmmakers are trying to achieve. This is the extraordinary sequence in which the ex-boxer, his career on the skids, is shown in the prison cell, slowly, methodically, and with increasing force, beating his head against the wall. This was something that De Niro had seen La Motta do in real life. It is the gesture of a defeated man who knows that he is the agent of his own misfortunes, but is powerless to stop himself from sliding closer to the abyss. La Motta is not articulate. Behind bars because he has been caught soliciting minors, vastly overweight, he is at his lowest ebb. He cannot express his feelings through words and so resorts to this primal, self-destructive behavior instead.

There is a pathos and majesty to De Niro's La Motta that is entirely absent in *Taxi Driver*. For all his self-scrutiny, Travis Bickle conspicuously fails to achieve any meaningful degree of self-knowledge. The highly ambiguous and ironic ending to the film, with Travis transformed into a folk hero and back grinning behind the wheel of his cab, shows just how deluded he remains. It also had one unlikely consequence: it paved the way for a sequel. Bizarrely, in early 2005, 30 years after the original, there was talk of resurrecting Travis. Robert De Niro gave an interview to the *New York Post* in which he acknowledged that he and Scorsese had had discussions about revisiting *Taxi Driver*. News agencies around the world picked up on the story.

The one problem was that the news did not seem to be true. "That's the downside of the internet. It's a totally spurious rumor—if the rumor is good enough, print it," Schrader commented in March 2005. "What happened was that four years ago, Scorsese, De Niro, and I met because Bob was thinking of doing it. We talked and I said I thought it was a terrible idea. Marty thought it was a bad idea. That was the end of the discussion. Every once in a while that rumor refloats, but it is just a terrible idea."

It was understandable why De Niro would be so keen to revisit *Taxi Driver*. In his early sixties, the actor seemed to be struggling to find roles that really stretched him. He had shown his flair for comedies in such projects as *Meet the Parents* (2000), *Meet the Fockers* (2004), and *Analyze This* (1999), but there had been many low points, perhaps most embarrassingly the animation/live-action fusion *The Adventures of Rocky and Bullwinkle* (2000), in which he had played opposite cartoon characters. (In a moment of dreadful self-parody, he had even rehashed his "Are you talkin' to me?" monologue.) There was a definite sense that his career was drifting.

For some time, it had been evident that De Niro craved fresh challenges. In 1993, he had made his directorial debut with *A Bronx Tale*, taken from a one-man play by Chazz Palminteri. In the film, De Niro plays a self-effacing bus driver who "gets up every morning to do a job he doesn't like very much but does it anyway for his family." As role model for his impressionable young son, he is contrasted with the flamboyant local gangster (Palminteri), who reads Machiavelli and advises the boy that it is better to be feared than to be loved.

A Bronx Tale was a very promising, if low-key, debut. Much of its color came from the Damon Runyon-like supporting cast, two-bit old-timers like Eddie Mush, with his pet slogan "If I didn't have bad luck, I wouldn't have any luck at all," and

JoJo the Whale, who is so obese he is rumored to have killed a dog by casting his vast shadow on it. De Niro showed an eye for comic detail, elicited a memorable performance from Palminteri, and squeezed both pathos and humor out of his original source material. The film was not successful and De Niro has not directed since. However, *Taxi Driver* was a project he was extraordinarily close to. According to Schrader, even before he read the screenplay, he had tried to write his own story about a young man who carried a gun around New York and fantasized about using it to kill diplomats at the UN building. Now, he was eager to revisit one of his greatest roles.

Hollywood studios have always been eager to make sequels if the potential box-office warrants it. There are many cases in which this has been done in the most cynical way, without any contribution from the filmmakers who devised the original material. Whether it be the long list of *Jaws* movies, or the *Rambo* films in which a character first portrayed in relatively serious fashion in Ted Kotcheff's *First Blood* (1980) was turned into a *Boys' Own* action hero, or *The Last Seduction II* (1999), a direct-to-video follow-up to John Dahl's 1994 thriller, recent Hollywood history is full of lousy sequels.

The reluctance of Scorsese and Schrader to embrace their lead actor's vision of a second coming of *Taxi Driver* was not surprising. In a sense, they had already made their own follow-up to *Taxi Driver* with *Bringing Out the Dead* (1999).

The relationship between director and writer had often been fractious. In 1976, in a long interview with *Film Comment*,

Schrader revealed how difficult the two found working together on *Taxi Driver*. "When I first saw the film, Marty and I had a talk about it; he ended up having an attack, screaming, accusing me of not knowing what the movie was about and of being against him. That's one of the things that may do him in. If he has a fall, it will be simply because certain flaws have been exaggerated by success—one of which is an inability to take criticism, a paranoia."

Peter Biskind's *Easy Riders, Raging Bulls*, chronicles the way that the friendship between Scorsese and Schrader began to fray. By the time they collaborated on *Raging Bull* (1980), both were using cocaine heavily. The dynamics of the relationship had shifted. As a filmmaker in his own right, not just a screenwriter, Schrader had increased status. He was not happy with the way that Scorsese and De Niro reworked his screenplay.

When they collaborated on *The Last Temptation of Christ* (1988), there was again tension. Scorsese had brought in his friend and frequent collaborator Jay Cocks to revise Schrader's screenplay, another source of bad feeling between the two men. They briefly considered a remake of Vincente Minnelli's 1952 melodrama about the inner workings of Hollywood, *The Bad and the Beautiful*, but this also ended in acrimony as the two men argued over who would take the script credit. As Schrader told the *Observer*, "I said to him [Scorsese], 'This is going to end up in one of two ways. Either the film is going to get made and we're going to become enemies, or the film is not going to get made and we'll stay friends. So let's just assume the latter is true and just quit. We've done three films. That's enough. We'll have dinner once a year.'"

Whatever the differences between the men, they had been resolved by the time they decided to work together on *Bringing Out the Dead* (1999), an adaptation of the book by New York paramedic Joe Connelly, who had spent eight years as an ambulance driver in New York.

The parallels between *Taxi Driver* and *Bringing Out the Dead* are self-evident. Both are about loners driving through the New York streets by night, roaming like lost souls. The overlap between the two films is made apparent right at the outset. Paramedic Frank Pierce (Nic Cage) is shown behind the wheel as Van Morrison's bluesy anthem 'TB Sheets' plays over the credits. There is a neon-lit close-up of Frank's eyes that clearly references the many similar shots of Travis Bickle. The voice-over narration is likewise a device that the films share. There is even the same steam billowing out of manholes on the streets.

"Saving someone's life is like falling in love, the best drug in the world," Frank tells us. "You wonder if you have become immortal. It's as if God has passed through you. Why deny it? God was you. But when things go wrong, spreading the blame is an essential medic survival tool: the family was crazy, the equipment broke, the patient smelled. The god of hellfire is not a role that anyone wants to play."

An intertitle tells us that the film is set in New York in the early 1990s. The timing is significant: this means before New York Mayor Rudolph Giuliani's so-called "zero tolerance" and "broken windows" policies helped clean up the streets. Just as in the city that Travis Bickle encountered 20 years before, there is evidence of decay, squalor, and corruption wherever you look. The hookers still clamor for trade on the sidewalks. The city seems permanently to be on the brink of apocalypse.

"The *Taxi Driver* comparison is there," Schrader admitted. "It's unavoidable. We had to make this feel like a bookend rather than a sequel. Travis Bickle wants to be alone: this character wants to be with somebody. This is a more adult version of those rolling emotions Marty and I felt 25 years ago." The difference now was that Scorsese and Schrader were "mellower." Moreover, Frank's instincts were the polar opposite to those of Travis. He may have been on a power jag, but he was trying to save people, not to shoot them into oblivion. Still, like Travis, he is a loner close to breaking point.

As the film begins, Frank and his hardbitten partner (played by the burly John Goodman) try to resuscitate a heart attack victim in a cramped New York apartment. They massage his chest and give him electric shocks, but the green line on their monitor stays obstinately flat. Frank is going through a bad patch. For months, he has not been able to save a single life. All he seems able to do is bear witness and "bring out the dead." He is a forlorn, exhausted figure. While his partner goes off to ring the hospital with details of another fatality, he asks the family to put on some music for the ailing man. Just as Frank Sinatra's 'September Of My Years' begins to blare out from the speakers, Frank gets a pulse. They bundle the man into the ambulance and rush him off to the hospital where, as usual, it is sheer bedlam. The man's daughter Mary (Patricia Arquette) tells Frank that he has "a face like a saint." The ambulance controller (voiced by

Scorsese) is barking out instructions of the next drive-by shooting and heart attacks.

Just as in *Taxi Driver*, Scorsese and Schrader are paying homage to Robert Bresson. The long-suffering Frank, ailing, unable to sleep, ready to take all the sins of the world on his shoulders, is a New York equivalent to the anguished priest in Bresson's *Diary of a Country Priest* (1951).

Frank's relationship with Mary echoes that between Travis and Iris in *Taxi Driver*. The difference here is that Mary does not have a pimp and is not a prostitute. She is an ex-addict. The father figure in her life is a Mephistophelian drug dealer who offers her the chance to blank out the problems of her everyday life. As in *Taxi Driver*, there is an almost Dickensian sentimentality about the way Scorsese portrays lost, innocent waifs. Not only does Frank fret over Mary, but he is also full of remorse over a homeless, teenage girl who died on his beat and whose face keeps appearing in front of him. There is no rhetoric here about a real rain to wash the scum off the sidewalk, but Scorsese still takes a voyeuristic interest in showing the underclass: New York's nighttime population of addicts and oddballs.

As a kid growing up in New York, he had witnessed such characters at first hand. To the confusion of the boy who harbored dreams of becoming a priest, he was told to ignore the suffering and squalor around him. "My parents wanted to protect my brother and myself from the horrors out there— the degradation of the poor derelicts, who were literally there on your block, in your building, on your stairs as you were going out to school in the morning; who were there drunk; fighting each other with broken bottles or knives, or dead, literally dead," Scorsese reflected. "Parents didn't want you to touch them—they're dirty, they're this, they're that. But at the same time, the church is always talking about compassion. So I've always had this split guilt: I've always felt not quite right not doing anything about it and that's one of the reasons I wanted to do this movie."

Scorsese embraced the project with the same fervor as he had *Taxi Driver*. "The film is episodic. but that's the nature of the paramedics' work," he told journalists. "I tried to do it according to how images hit me when I was riding in those ambulances. I undercranked the camera a lot. In order to drive like that, you have to be driven. You want to save lives. You've got to be like a solider to go out there."

Ostensibly based on real-life incidents, *Bringing Out the Dead* is every bit as Baroque and stylized as *Taxi Driver*, full of slow motion, dream sequences, elaborate camera movements, long-running tracking shots, plenty of morbid humor, and lots of blood. This is a frenetic, hyper-charged film. There is a certain pathos in the way that Scorsese and Schrader, both well into their fifties, try to recapture the relentless energy and edge they had brought to *Taxi Driver*. Inevitably, it is a forlorn endeavor. Somehow, the magic was not quite there. Cage was a fine actor. He researched his role meticulously, going out on call with New York paramedics, but he was not a De Niro. Scorsese had had many imitators over the years. Here, he was copying himself, albeit in bravura fashion.

At times, this even seemed like *Taxi Driver* in reverse. Instead of Travis massacring the pimps, it showed Frank achieving an unlikely redemption by saving the life of the drug dealer, impaled on a metal fence high up in a New York skyscraper. Beneath the gallows humor, there are even hints of a perverse nostalgia. Scorsese is paying tribute to a New York that no longer exists (and that some would say never really had outside his imagination). The city is portrayed in a similar light in his unsettling screwball comedy *After Hours* (1985), in which Griffin Dunne plays Paul Hackett, a New Yorker with a steady job and a regulated, monotonous lifestyle. He meets a young woman (Rosanna Arquette) in a restaurant, takes her telephone number, later calls her, and arranges to meet her, but what should be a routine date goes very badly wrong. As if he is a character in a Kafka novel, he is confronted with a nightmarish world in which logic no longer applies. He loses his money and then looks on with bemusement as he encounters an array of New York grotesques: psychotic and suicidal women, punks, oddball sculptors, and vigilantes. Yet again, Scorsese turns his home city into a phantasmagoric world in which normal, bourgeois life is banished to the margins.

In 1976, *Taxi Driver* hit a nerve and became an unlikely box-office success. *Bringing Out the Dead* (1999) failed to capture the imagination in the same way. After costume dramas like 1993's *Age of Innocence*, epic gangster films like 1995's *Casino*, and a foray into Buddhism with *Kundun* in 1997, he now proved that he could still recapture the old intensity. He lost none of his flair for making adrenalin-driven urban morality tales. The difference here was that there was no Travis Bickle—and no De Niro to play him.

The one film of the 1990s that did match the warped intensity of *Taxi Driver*, and that belatedly compensated

Harvey Keitel for missing out on the role as Travis all those years before, was Abel Ferrara's dirty cop drama *The Bad Lieutenant* (1992). Ferrara is one of the more shambolic figures in recent American film history. The Bronx-born Italian-American director first sprang to prominence (or at least notoriety) with his 1979 effort *The Driller Killer*, which itself can be seen as a companion piece to *Taxi Driver*. The setting is again a New York coming apart at the seams. If anything, the city of *Driller Killer* is even more ragged around the edges than that shown in *Taxi Driver*. Ferrara even provides an equivalent of Travis Bickle in the shape of an artist (played by the director himself) who is so disoriented and enraged by the noise and commotion around him that he goes on a murderous rampage of his own, albeit with a pneumatic drill rather than a .44 Magnum.

The gangster Christopher Walken plays in Ferrara's *The King of New York* (1989) also seems like a cousin of Travis Bickle. Frank White is a gangster with a social conscience. Through his cocaine deals, he aims to earn enough to improve the city's crumbling medical facilities. Like Travis, Frank is an inscrutable character, part sleazebag, part martyr. Ferrara hurls in even more references to Catholicism than are found in *Mean Streets* (1973) and takes a perverse relish in contrasting images of urban squalor and violence with moments of quiet religious symbolism. There are several, seemingly unmotivated cutaways to a statue of the Virgin Mary. Ferrara gives Frank quite a send-off. The taxis are gridlocked, the rain is lashing down, and a hundred policemen swarm around the dying gangster, as if they are his supplicants and he really is their king.

If Scorsese flirts with the dark side of New York life, Ferrara embraces it whole-heartedly. *The Bad Lieutenant*, not only his best but arguably his most coherent film, is a dark yarn about a New York cop who has taken venality to new extremes. The lieutenant (Keitel) has a holy trinity of addictions: booze, crack, and heroin. He finds gambling pretty hard to resist, too, and is in hock to the bookies for far more than he can afford.

The film was inspired by a real-life incident in 1982 when a nun was raped in Spanish Harlem. The plot hinges on the lieutenant's erratic attempts to bring the rapists to justice. It is also a story of redemption. Ferrara's project is to steep the lieutenant in squalor and sin as far as he will go and then to allow him a saving moment of grace. Predictably, Ferrara ran into problems with censors. (Not even Scorsese had shown scenes as extreme as nuns being gang-raped in a church.) However, Keitel's performance earned plaudits wherever it was shown. With the scenes of the lieutenant naked and wailing his sins, this was a performance of extraordinary rawness and intensity. There was also a gravitas about it that neither Keitel nor De Niro could have matched at the time of *Taxi Driver*. The fact that Keitel was now in middle age, paunchy and weatherbeaten, enabled him to bring real pathos to a character who at first glance seems utterly despicable.

In hindsight, Travis Bickle seems like a prototype not just for the equally weird and warped protagonists of Ferrara's movies, but also for many other characters who have appeared in Scorsese's subsequent films. What Travis craves is attention. The same desire to be noticed drives Rupert

Pupkin, the mediocre comedian played by De Niro in *The King of Comedy* (1982). Like Travis, sitting in his taxi and staring at Betsy through the windows of Senator Palantine's campaign headquarters, Rupert is the outsider looking in at a world he wants to gatecrash. In Rupert Pupkin's case, the quarry is Jerry Langford (Jerry Lewis), a chatshow host and comedian whose program Pupkin is desperate to appear on. In *Taxi Driver*, Travis becomes a folk hero by instigating a massacre. In *The King of Comedy*, the equally deranged and driven Pupkin transforms himself into a celebrity by kidnapping Langford, the man he ostensibly admires, and threatening to kill him unless he hands over the reins of his show for a night.

If *Taxi Driver* tapped into an anger and paranoia that Scorsese was feeling at the time he made it, *The King of Comedy* caught the drive and ambition of the young director. True, Scorsese did not resort to kidnap to further his career, but he would do just about anything else to catch the eyes of Hollywood. In the early 1970s, when he was trying to get a foothold in the industry, he acknowledged, he was ready to flatter, cajole, browbeat, and even intimidate anyone who might have been in a position to help him. "It's the same way I made my first pictures, with no money and constant rejection—going back and back and back until finally, somehow, you get a lucky break. Actually luck doesn't have that much to do with it; it's just this constant battering away at this monolith. Pupkin goes about it the wrong way but he does have drive. I remember I'd go any place, do anything. I'd try to get into screenings, get into any kind of social situation to talk up projects," Scorsese admitted.

Ray Liotta's Henry Hill in *Goodfellas* (1990) was another Scorsese protagonist craving recognition and respect. "As far back as I can remember," Liotta's voice-over begins, "I'd always wanted to be a gangster ... to be a somebody in a neighborhood full of nobodies." The bravura ending of the film, in which a paranoid, coked-up Henry runs errands, tries to cook a tomato sauce, delivers guns to Jimmy Conway, and drives stressed through town with police helicopters hovering above him, has the same warped, manic feel as much of *Taxi Driver*. (Contemporary accounts suggest that Scorsese was just as wired himself during the *Taxi Driver* shoot.)

The bloodletting at the end of *Taxi Driver* seemed to free Scorsese. He no longer had any qualms about depicting violence. *Goodfellas* opens in horrific fashion with the mobsters stabbing the still living, still squirming body of Billy Batts in the boot of their car. We discover subsequently that the knife Tommy De Vito is brandishing so enthusiastically was taken from his mother's dinner table. The scene is repulsive, but is played in matter-of-fact fashion. Killing was an everyday fact of life for these characters. Audiences, critics, and censors were no longer surprised to see such a scene in a Scorsese movie. In his work, they knew, it came with the territory.

In *Cape Fear* (1991), De Niro offered what might best be described as a pantomime villain version of Travis Bickle. His character, the tattoo-covered redneck stalking the lawyer who put him behind bars for rape, is an über-psychopath. He even speaks in the same biblical language as Travis: "I am like God and God like me. I am as large as God, He as small as I. He cannot above me, nor I beneath him be."

If reverberations from *Taxi Driver* were to be felt again and again in its director's later work, the film's influence also stretched in some other, often surprising directions. *Taxi Driver* was released in 1976, just as punk music was beginning to hit its stride in Britain and the US. Travis Bickle became an icon for the movement. His pre-massacre look of army jacket and mohawk haircut was imitated by kids on both sides of the Atlantic. British band The Clash was especially enthusiastic. Singer-songwriter Joe Strummer quoted Travis's monologues at length in 'Red Angel Dragnet,' one of the tracks on the band's 1982 album *Combat Rock*. Strummer even started sporting a Travis-like mohawk himself. Scorsese reciprocated his admiration, giving the band walk-on parts in *The King of Comedy* (1982).

Europeans warmed to *Taxi Driver* even more than Americans. When the film won the Palme D'Or in Cannes, it was seen as exposing the rotten underbelly of a society still suffering from the twin traumas of Watergate and the Vietnam War. It also chimed with the equally dark films about disaffected outsiders being made during the same period by the prolific Rainer Werner Fassbinder.

Over the years, many European filmmakers would cite *Taxi Driver* as one of their great inspirations. The most extreme and twisted homage to Scorsese came from the French director Gaspar Noe in his extraordinary 1998 debut feature *Seul Contre Tous*. The protagonist Jean Chevalier (brilliantly played by Philippe Nahon) is a down-at-mouth, depressed butcher, just out of jail, without work or money, who vows revenge against "the nigger faggots" and "faggots in suits" he blames for his plight. Although the film seems to be a realist drama, exposing social problems in late 1990s France, Noe's interest was less in unemployment, racism, and the rise of the right than in making a phantasmagoric psycho-drama about a Travis Bickle-like outsider.

Travis was also an inspiration to a new wave of independent US filmmakers who emerged in the 1990s. Quentin Tarantino, the leading figure in US indie cinema of the period, cited *Taxi Driver* as one of his favorite films. His screenplay for Oliver Stone's *Natural Born Killers* (1994) explored some of the same themes, most notably the way in which the US media make celebrities out of killers and psychopaths. Mickey and Mallory (Woody Harrelson and Juliette Lewis) kill roughly 50 people. Stone provoked an outrage by saying that this was not such a big deal in a century in which at least 100 million people died violent deaths. Nonetheless, it was apparent that no new Hollywood film was ever likely to match the impact of *Taxi Driver*. In the years since it had been made, the culture had changed. The 1990s were a decade of postmodern irony and cynicism. David Fincher's *Fight Club* (1999) tapped some of the same rage and violence that had fed into *Taxi Driver*. It, too, exposed the seething discontents that simmered under the surface of placid middle-class American life, but it was too knowing, too clever, too full of self-reflexive tics to have the universality of appeal of *Taxi Driver*. Meanwhile, Tony Scott's *True Romance* (1993), scripted by Tarantino, seemed like *Taxi Driver* done as a romantic comedy. It is a tall tale about a geekish, Travis Bickle-like video store assistant from Detroit (Christian Slater as the Tarantino-like Clarence) who blithely leaves a trail of dead bodies—including that of his own father—in his wake. There is the same bloodshed, the same alienation, but this time, it is played for laughs.

While *Taxi Driver* fed into the films of a generation of would-be Scorseses, eager to express their anger and disgust at the world around them, it also became appropriated by the Hollywood money-making machine. Over the years, Travis Bickle was marketed with almost as much energy as Mickey Mouse. Scorsese had not thought much of the original poster for *Taxi Driver*. It showed a black and white full-length still of De Niro as Travis walking head bowed, hands in pockets, down the sidewalk. "On every street in every city, there's a nobody who dreams of being a somebody," ran the tag line beneath his feet. De Niro's name was above the title. A porno theater can be seen behind him offering, in block capitals, "ADULT MOVIES with LIVE SEX." One or two figures are visible in the deep background, but otherwise Travis is all alone.

The poster was an advertising cliché. This kind of image of the good-looking man with the sullen demeanor striding through the forbidding city could just as well have been used to sell jeans to adolescents who also yearned "to be a somebody." If you did not know the context, you would imagine that this was a man who had broken up with his girlfriend or lost someone close to him. He appeared to be grieving. There was little hint he was a psychopath. That, perhaps, explains why the image was so readily embraced. "The studio made a B-movie poster, just black and white, Bob De Niro walking down Eighth Avenue, a porn theater behind him ... I hated that poster but it was the one that sold the picture," Scorsese admitted. "So it behoves me to listen to people about marketing."

Largely thanks to George Lucas's *Star Wars* (1977), the 1970s was the decade that ushered in merchandizing of movies on a huge scale. On the face of it, *Taxi Driver* would seem the least likely film to benefit from the new-found fad for tie-in toys and products, but in the three decades since the film was made, there has been a surprisingly brisk trade in *Taxi Driver* T-shirts, posters, and (by the beginning of the internet era) mouse pads. Travis's "Are you talkin' to me?" monologue was borrowed by comedians and satirists and soon lost its power to shock.

Meanwhile, the film itself was accepted by the mainstream. In 1996, when the American Film Institute published a list of the 100 greatest movies of all time (as chosen by "1500 leaders of the American movie community'), *Taxi Driver* came in at number 47, an unlikely achievement given Hollywood's revulsion for the project when the filmmakers were first trying to finance it. A film that had been called "incoherent," "misogynistic," and even "fascistic" was firmly ensconced in the canon alongside *Citizen Kane* (1941), *Casablanca* (1942), *The Godfather*, (1972) et al.

Scorsese often hints that he has made a Faustian pact with the Hollywood studios. For him, as for so many of the filmmakers he most admires, he simultaneously works within the system and against it. As he observed in his 1997 documentary *A Personal Journey Through American Movies*, the debate between art and commerce was neverending. "What does it take to be a filmmaker in Hollywood?" he asked. "Even today I still wonder what it takes to be a professional or even an artist in Hollywood. How do you survive the constant tug of war between commercial expression and personal imperatives? What is the price you pay to work in Hollywood? Do you end up with a split personality? Do you make one movie for them, one for yourselves?"

On the face of it, his 2004 feature *The Aviator* was "one for them." This was not a personal project that he had nurtured for decades like *The Last Temptation of Christ* (1988) or *Gangs of New York* (2002). It was a film he had "inherited" when the original director Michael Mann had stepped down. However, scrape beneath the surface of this opulent, expensive biopic about the tycoon and it becomes apparent that the themes are very familiar. It is stretching it a bit to call Hughes (played by Leonardo DiCaprio) a mogul version of Travis Bickle—the two characters are clearly at the opposite ends of the scale of success, and one is fictional and the other real—but the overlaps are self-evident. *The Aviator* was yet another Scorsese film about an outsider desperate to be noticed. Katharine Hepburn is his Betsy. The scenes in which Hughes is humiliated by her preppy, East Coast family recall those in which Travis is all at sea in Senator Palantine's headquarters. Hughes (at least as portrayed by DiCaprio) has that same combustible mix of charm and menace that made Travis so memorable. What was more, like Travis, he was some kind of nutcase. The eccentric recluse who kept his urine in bottles and became terrified about bad hygiene was not so very different from the 26-year-old Vietnam vet turned taxi driver, alone in his apartment, scribbling his doom-laden diary and strapping himself up with weapons, ready for the final battle. Late in his career, when he is one of Hollywood's senior statesmen, it seems that Scorsese cannot escape the specter of his most memorable creation.

For De Niro, too, there is a sense that Travis Bickle is still the role that defines his career. In late 2004, a new advertising campaign, "My Life, My Card," was launched for a well-known credit card (American Express). The black and white print ad shows De Niro standing opposite Jay Street in Brooklyn. His back is to camera, but his head is tilted to the right so that we can see his profile. He is wearing a large great coat that is billowing in the breeze. Just as he was in 1975 when he shot *Taxi Driver*, he is still the man alone. On the left of the image, a yellow cab is driving away. The streets are damp from recent rain. Steam is rising from a manhole. In the distance, we can see tenement buildings, a fire escape, a few people loitering on the other side of the road, and the lights that a movie crew have set up. It is a quintessential New York image. It is also consciously playing on memories of De Niro's New York-made movies, *Taxi Driver* in particular. Scorsese was commissioned to oversee the creative campaign. In 1975, when they were making *Taxi Driver*, the director and his lead actor were prepared to all but waive their fees to get the movie made. Looking at the American Express ad, it is impossible not to be reminded of the *Taxi Driver* ad, with its slogan "On every street in every city, there's a nobody who dreams of being a somebody."

To accompany the print image, Scorsese shot a TV commercial showing De Niro walking around New York and explaining why the city means so much to him. Given that American Express sponsors the Tribeca Festival, the event De Niro set up in 2002 in the wake of 9/11, it is understandable why he was willing to take what seemed like the kind of hack, commercial assignment he would always have resisted in the past. Whatever the circumstances, there is something strangely poignant about De Niro back roaming the streets of New York, again under the guidance of Scorsese.

For Schrader, the third soul in the *Taxi Driver* trinity, there must be a sense of deja vu about the battles he has been obliged to fight again and again to get his subsequent movies made or shown. Just as with his *Taxi Driver* script in the early 1970s, he found himself being buffeted around by studios, distributors, and producers. His Russell Banks adaptation, *Affliction* (1998), about a middle-aged, divorced, Midwestern type (Nick Nolte) who shares many of Travis Bickle's neuroses, was spurned when it was first completed. No one in the US wanted to release it. When finally it was shown in the movie theaters, critics warmed to it ("a magnificent feel-bad movie," wrote one) and James Coburn, who plays Nolte's bullying martinet of a father, ended up winning a Best Supporting Actor Oscar.

Schrader had to wait equally long for vindication when he directed a prequel to William Friedkin's *The Exorcist* (1973). The movie was already complete when his bosses at Morgan Creek sacked him, took the footage away, and hired another director to make a new version. For a while, it looked as if Schrader was going to suffer the humiliation of seeing his version shelved. The problem, it was alleged, was that Schrader's *Exorcist* simply was not bloody enough to appeal to teen audiences. "If you have made a film which has been shelved or discarded, nobody—not your wife or best friend—will believe it is any good because they [Hollywood studios] don't discard $35 million investments," the crestfallen filmmaker lamented. In the end, Morgan Creek did relent. Schrader's movie received mixed to favorable notices. Schrader has had his successes, but as the whole grim saga underlined, the original creator of Travis Bickle was still being treated as a pariah.

Whatever the vicissitudes of their subsequent careers, Scorsese, De Niro, and Schrader all know that *Taxi Driver* is as good a film as they could have made with the elements at their disposal. "I know that *Taxi Driver* holds up," Schrader says today. "The reason it holds up is that it is the real deal. Scorsese, Bob [De Niro], and I were in that place at that time."

postscript

Travis brought back to life

Shoot the President, become a folk hero. One of the themes Paul Schrader explored in his *Taxi Driver* screenplay was that strange habit US culture has of turning its rogues into full-blown national celebrities. Whether Lincoln's assassin John Wilkes Booth or Charles Manson (the man behind the Sharon Tate murders), or John Brown (who orchestrated a massacre in the name of his anti-slavery campaign) or Travis Bickle's forefather, the bungling, would-be killer Arthur Bremer, American popular history is full of men fondly remembered for their bloody misdeeds. The villains become identifiable brand names.

In May 2005, Sony Pictures revealed its unlikely plans to revive Travis Bickle. The alienated, trigger-happy outsider first brought to life by Scorsese, De Niro and Schrader was to become an animated figure in a brand new *Taxi Driver* computer game. The plan was to launch the game in 2006, to commemorate the 30th anniversary of the original release of the film. Sony was partnering with the Majesco Entertainment Company on the new venture

On their official press releases announcing the new project, neither Sony nor Majesco made more than passing reference to Scorsese, Schrader and De Niro. As the releases acknowledged, *Taxi Driver* was "a brutally compelling portrayal of alienation and psychoses," but it was pretty clear that the new computer game was not going to be marketed on the back of Travis Bickle's schizophrenia. Nor was it likely to acknowledge his overt racism.

"Nominated for four Academy Awards, *Taxi Driver* remains one of the most iconoclastic films of our time. Compelling and powerful, the movie ensnares viewers in the seedy urban world of New York cabbie Travis Bickle, and we hope to do likewise with our game," declared Ken Gold, Majesco's Vice-Preisdent of Marketing. "We look forward to developing a game that remains true to the spirit and style of the movie, and embodies a total entertainment experience."

The phrase "a total entertainment experience" couldn't help but ring a little hollow. In Hollywood films of 2004/2005, for instance Robert Rodriguez and Frank Miller's *Sin City*, the violence and squalor Scorsese had shown for real in *Taxi Driver* had become almost a fashion statement.

Sin City, based on Frank Miller's graphic novels, was full of alienated, Travis Bickle-like loners. It touched on many of the same themes as *Taxi Driver*: voyeurism, prostitution, paedophilia, vigilante-style revenge and political corruption among them. The opening of the film, in which Hartigan (Bruce Willis) goes all guns blazing to the protection of an 11-year-old girl, isn't so very different from the massacre at the end of *Taxi Driver*, when Travis Bickle murders the pimps in his bid to save Iris. Both movies make heavy use of voiceover.

The difference, though, was that in *Sin City* the horror is now hidden behind thick layers of irony, artifice and glamour. As much blood gushes here as in *Taxi Driver*, but the filmmakers have gone even further in desaturating the colours so the most violent scenes are mildly less shocking.

The film is shot noir-style in monochrome, with occasional flashes of colour. Bizarrely, the blood is white. Whenever a limb is lopped off or someone is shot, it's as if there is milk bursting from their veins. A bravura piece of filmmaking, *Sin City* also an adolescent male's wish fulfillment fantasy. It is not weighed down in the slightest by any of the religious soul-searching or political awareness that has always characterised the work of Schrader and Scorsese.

What had made *Taxi Driver* so unsettling was the gulf between Travis Bickle's inflated sense of himself as chivalric and heroic city avenger and the reality that he was a socially inept outsider with a lousy job and a craving for junk food and pornography. It is very hard to see how any *Taxi Driver* computer game could address this contradiction without losing the audience at which it is bound primarily to be marketed: namely adolescent males.

In 2004/2005, Hollywood studios had begun ransacking their back catalogues, looking for movies they could customise as computer games. On one level, this was just a natural extension to the spin-off marketing and merchandising which had long accompanied any major release. The downside was that the intentions of the artists who created the original works were invariably overridden.

Francis Coppola refused to endorse to a video game of *The Godfather*. His actors had less scruples. Shortly before his death, Marlon Brando expressed his enthusiasm at the idea of becoming a videogame star. "I could lend my voice and acting skills to a role without having to be physically on set," the reclusive actor was quoted as saying in trade paper Variety.

Clint Eastwood gave his blessing (and lent his voice and likeness) to a video game of *Dirty Harry*. Sean Connery did the same for a video game of *From Russia With Love*. Al Pacino lent his likeness (though not his voice) to a *Scarface* video game. At the time of writing, it is yet to be confirmed whether De Niro or any of his fellow cast members will be involved in the new *Taxi Driver* project.

Such ventures can't help but bowdlerise the films on which they are based. *Taxi Driver* was made (and set) in a specific city at a specific time. Not even the most brilliant games designers would have a chance of recapturing the reality of life on the streets of New York in that sweltering summer of 1975. If you weren't there, you weren't there.

appendix 1

Taxi Driver Credits (*USA 1976*)

Directed by
Martin Scorsese

Screenplay
Paul Schrader

Cast (in credits order)
Robert De Niro .... Travis Bickle
Cybill Shepherd .... Betsy
Peter Boyle .... Wizard
Jodie Foster .... Iris Steensma
Harvey Keitel .... 'Sport' Matthew
Leonard Harris .... Senator Charles Palantine
Albert Brooks .... Tom
rest of cast listed alphabetically:
Diahnne Abbott .... Concession girl
Frank Adu .... Angry black man
Gino Ardito .... Policeman at rally
Victor Argo .... Melio (as Vic Argo)
Garth Avery .... Iris' friend
Harry Cohn .... Cabbie in Bellmore
Copper Cunningham .... Hooker in cab
Brenda Dickson-Weinberg .... Soap opera woman
   (as Brenda Dickson)

Harry Fischler .... Dispatcher

Nat Grant .... Stickup man

Richard Higgs .... Tall Secret Service man

Beau Kayser .... Soap opera man

Victor Magnotta .... Secret Service photographer
  (as Vic Magnotta)

Bob Maroff .... Mafioso

Norman Matlock .... Charlie T

Bill Minkin .... Tom's assistant

Murray Moston .... Iris' timekeeper

Harry Northup .... Doughboy

Gene Palma .... Street drummer

Carey Poe .... Campaign worker

Steven Prince .... Andy (gun salesman)

Peter Savage .... The john

Martin Scorsese .... Homicidal passenger in Travis' cab

Nicholas Shields .... Palantine's aide

Ralph S. Singleton .... TV interviewer (as Ralph Singleton)

Joe Spinell .... Personnel officer

Maria Turner .... Angry hooker

Robin Utt .... Campaign worker

William Donovan .... Police officer (uncredited)

Jean Elliott .... Clerk at Sam Goody store (uncredited)

Jason Holt .... Extra (uncredited)

Debbi Morgan .... Girl at Columbus Circle (uncredited)

Billie Perkins .... Friend of Iris (uncredited)

Harlan Cary Poe .... Campaign worker (uncredited)

Production Companies:
Columbia Pictures presents an Italo-Judeo production/A
Bill/Phillips production/A Martin Scorsese film

Produced by
Julia Phillips
Michael Phillips

Associate Producer
Phillip M. Goldfarb

Original Music by
Bernard Herrmann

Cinematography by
Michael Chapman

Film Editing by
Tom Rolf
Melvin Shapiro

Casting by
Juliet Taylor

Art Direction by
Charles Rosen

Set Decoration by
Herbert F. Mulligan   (as Herbert Mulligan)

Costume Design by
Ruth Morley

Makeup Department
Irving Buchman .... makeup artist
Mona Orr .... hair stylist
Dick Smith .... special makeup

Production Management
Phillip M. Goldfarb .... production manager (uncredited)

Second Unit Director or Assistant Director
Robert P. Cohen .... DGA trainee (as Robert Cohen)
William Eustace .... second assistant director
Peter R. Scoppa .... assistant director
Ralph S. Singleton .... second assistant director
   (as Ralph Singleton)

Art Department
Leslie Bloom .... property master (as Les Bloom)
Dave Goodonoff .... assistant property master
   (as Dave Goodnoff)
Cosmo Sorice .... scenic artist

Sound Department
Rick Alexander .... sound re-recording mixer
   (as Dick Alexander)
Gordon Davidson .... sound effects editor
James Fritch .... sound effects editor (as Jim Fritch)
Sam Gemette .... sound effects editor

David M. Horton .... sound effects editor (as David Hourton)
Les Lazarowitz .... sound mixer
Roger Pietschmann .... sound recordist
Vern Poore .... sound re-recording mixer
Robert Rogow .... boom operator
Tex Rudloff .... sound re-recording supervisor
Frank E. Warner .... supervising sound effects editor
Shinichi Yamazaki .... music editor

Special Effects by
Tony Parmelee .... special effects

Visual Effects by
David Nichols .... visual consultant

Other crew
Keith Addis .... assistant to producers
Keith Addis .... lyricist
Marion Billings .... special publicist
Jackson Browne .... singer
Julia Cameron .... special thanks
Kay Chapin .... script supervisor
Al Craine .... wardrober
Loretta Cubberley .... special thanks
Pat Dodos .... secretary to the producers
Jerry Drange .... special thanks
Sylvia Fay .... atmosphere casting (as Sylvia Faye)
Connie Foster .... double: Jodie Foster
Richard B. Goodwin .... special thanks (as Richard Goodwin)
Raymond Hartwick .... transportation coordinator (as Ray Hartwick)

Jack Hayer .... special thanks

Bernard Herrmann .... thanks

Alec Hirschfeld .... assistant camera

Amy Holden Jones .... assistant to director (as Amy Jones)

Eugene Iemola .... production assistant

Bill Johnson .... assistant camera

Linda Kopcyk .... special thanks

Kris Kristofferson .... special thanks

Marcia Lucas .... supervising editor

Charlie McCarthy .... special thanks

Howard Newman .... publicist

Dan Perri .... title designer

Hank Phillippi .... special thanks

Richard Quinlan .... gaffer

Ed Quinn .... grip (as Edward Quinn)

Noni Rock .... production office coordinator

Renate Rupp .... secretary to the producers

Fred Schuler .... camera operator

Steve Shapiro .... special photography

Chris Soldo .... production assistant

Gary Springer .... production assistant

George Trirogoff .... assistant editor

Robert Ward .... key grip

William Ward .... best boy (as Billy Ward)

Billy Weber .... assistant editor (as William Weber)

Josh Weiner .... still photographer

Sandra Weintraub .... creative consultant

Ron Zarilla .... assistant camera

Michael Zingale .... camera operator: second unit

appendix 2

Martin Scorsese filmography

The Departed (2006) *(filming)*
The Aviator (2004)
Gangs of New York (2002)
Bringing Out the Dead (1999)
My Voyage to Italy (1999)
Kundun (1997)
Casino (1995)
The Age of Innocence (1993)
Cape Fear (1991)
Goodfellas (1990)
Made in Milan (1990)
New York Stories (1989) (segment "Life Lessons")
The Last Temptation of Christ (1988)
Bad (1987)
The Color of Money (1986)
After Hours (1985)
The King of Comedy (1983)
Raging Bull (1980)
The Last Waltz (1978)
New York, New York (1977)
Taxi Driver (1976)
Alice Doesn't Live Here Anymore (1974)
Italianamerican (1974)
Mean Streets (1973)

Boxcar Bertha (1972)

Street Scenes 1970 (1970)

Who's That Knocking at My Door (1967)

The Big Shave (1967)

It's Not Just You, Murray! (1964)

What's a Nice Girl Like You Doing in a Place Like This? (1963)

Vesuvius VI (1959)

appendix 3

Robert De Niro filmography

Hide and Seek (2005)
The Bridge Of San Luis Rey (2004)
Meet The Fockers (2004)
Shark Tale (voice) (2004)
Godsend (2004)
Analyze That (2002)
City By the Sea (2002)
Showtime (2002)
The Score (2001)
Fifteen Minutes (2001)
Meet The Parents (2000)
Men Of Honor (2000)
The Adventures Of Rocky & Bullwinkle (2000)
Flawless (1999)
Analyze This (1998)
Ronin (1998)
Cop Land (1997)
Great Expectations (1997)
Jackie Brown (1997)
Wag The Dog (1997)
The Fan (1996)
Marvin's Room (1996)
Sleepers (1996)
Casino (1995)

Heat (1995)

Les Cent Et Une Nuits (1995)

Mary Shelley's Frankenstein (1994)

A Bronx Tale (1993)

Mad Dog And Glory (1993)

This Boy's Life (1993)

Night And The City (1992)

Backdraft (1991)

Cape Fear (1991)

Guilty By Suspicion (1991)

Mistress (1991)

Awakenings (1990)

Goodfellas (1990)

Stanley And Iris (1990)

Jacknife (1989)

We're No Angels (1989)

Midnight Run (1988)

Angel Heart (1987)

The Untouchables (1987)

The Mission (1986)

Brazil (1985)

Falling In Love (1984)

Once Upon A Time In America (1984)

King Of Comedy (1982)

True Confessions (1981)

Raging Bull (1980)

The Deer Hunter (1978)

New York, New York (1977)

The Last Tycoon (1976)

1900 (1976)

Taxi Driver (1976)
The Godfather Part 2 (1974)
Bang The Drum Slowly (1973)
Mean Streets (1973)
The Gang That Couldn't Shoot Straight (1971)
Jennifer On My Mind (1971)
Born To Win (1971)
The Swap (1971)
Bloody Mama (1970)
Hi, Mom! (1970)
The Wedding Party (1969)
Greetings (1968)
Three Rooms In Manhattan (1965)

appendix 4

Cybill Sheperd filmography

Open Window (2005)
Marine Life (2000)
Journey of the Heart (1997)
The Last Word (1995)
Once Upon a Crime... (1992)
Married to It (1991)
Alice (1990)
Texasville (1990)
Chances Are (1989)
The Return (1980)
Americathon (1979)
The Lady Vanishes (1979)
Silver Bears (1978)
Special Delivery (1976)
Taxi Driver (1976)
At Long Last Love (1975)
Daisy Miller (1974)
The Heartbreak Kid (1972)
The Last Picture Show (1971)

appendix 5

Harvey Keitel filmography

Go Go Tales (2005)
One Last Dance (2005)
Shadows in the Sun (2005)
Be Cool (2005)
The Bridge of San Luis Rey (2004)
National Treasure (2004)
Dreaming of Julia (2003)
Who Killed the Idea? (2003)
The Galindez File (2003)
Crime Spree (2003)
Puerto Vallarta Squeeze (2003)
Beeper (2002)
Red Dragon (2002)
Ginostra (2002)
Nowhere (2002)
The Grey Zone (2001)
Taking Sides (2001)
Vipera (2001)
Nailed (2001)
Little Nicky (2000)
Prince of Central Park (2000)
U-571 (2000)
Presence of Mind (1999)
Holy Smoke (1999)

Three Seasons (1999)

My West (1998)

Finding Graceland (1998)

Lulu on the Bridge (1998)

Shadrach (1998)

FairyTale: A True Story (1997)

Cop Land (1997)

City of Industry (1997)

Head Above Water (1996)

From Dusk Till Dawn (1996)

Blue in the Face (1995)

Clockers (1995)

Ulysses' Gaze (1995)

Smoke (1995)

Imaginary Crimes (1994)

Pulp Fiction (1994)

Somebody to Love (1994)

Monkey Trouble (1994)

Dangerous Game (1993)

Rising Sun (1993)

The Piano (1993)

Point of No Return (1993)

The Young Americans (1993)

Bad Lieutenant (1992)

Sister Act (1992)

Reservoir Dogs (1992)

Bugsy (1991)

Thelma & Louise (1991)

Mortal Thoughts (1991)

The Two Jakes (1990)

Two Evil Eyes (1990)
The Battle of the Three Kings (1990)
January Man (1989)
The Last Temptation of Christ (1988)
Caro Gorbaciov
The Pick-up Artist (1987)
The Inquiry (1987)
The Men's Club (1986)
Wise Guys (1986)
Off Beat (1986)
Camorra (1986)
Blindside (1986)
The American Bride (1986)
Nemo (1984)
Falling in Love (1984)
Exposed (1983)
Order of Death (1983)
A Stone in the Mouth (1983)
That Night in Varennes (1982)
The Border (1982)
Bad Timing (1980)
Deathwatch (1980)
Saturn 3 (1980)
Eagle's Wing (1979)
Fingers (1978)
Blue Collar (1978)
The Duellists (1977)
Welcome to L.A. (1976)
Buffalo Bill and the Indians (1976)
Mother, Jugs & Speed (1976)

Taxi Driver (1976)

That's the Way of the World (1975)

Alice Doesn't Live Here Anymore (1974)

Mean Streets (1973)

Who's That Knocking at My Door (1967)

Reflections in a Golden Eye (1967)

appendix 6

Jodie Foster filmography

A Very Long Engagement (2004)
Panic Room (2002)
The Dangerous Lives Of Altar Boys (2002)
Anna And The King (1999)
Contact (1997)
Maverick (1994)
Nell (1994)
Sommersby (1993)
Shadows And Fog (1992)
Little Man Tate (1991)
The Silence Of The Lambs (1991)
Catchfire (1989)
The Accused (1988)
Stealing Home (1988)
Siesta (1987)
Five Corners (1987)
Mesmerized (1986)
The Blood Of Others (1984)
The Hotel New Hampshire (1984)
Svengali (TV) (1983)
O'Hara's Wife (1982)
Carny (1980)
Foxes (1980)
Candleshoe (1977)

Il Casotto (1977)

Moi, Fleur Bleue (1977)

The Little Girl Who Lives Down The Lane (1976)

Freaky Friday (1976)

Bugsy Malone (1976)

Taxi Driver (1976)

Echoes Of A Summer (1976)

Alice Doesn't Live Here Anymore (1974)

One Little Indian (1973)

Tom Sawyer (1973)

Kansas City Bomber (1972)

Napoleon And Samantha (1972)

index